how2become

How to become a
A UK SOLICITOR

w   n

D0995842

T0479

Orders: Please contact How2become Ltd, Suite 2, 50 Churchill Square Business Centre, Kings Hill, Kent ME19 4YU.

You can order through Amazon.co.uk under ISBN, via the website www.How2Become.com or through Gardners.com.

ISBN: 978-1910202296

First published 2015

Disclaimer

Every effort has been made to ensure that the information contained within this guide is accurate at the time of publication. How2become Ltd are not responsible for anyone failing any part of any selection process as a result of the information contained within this guide. How2become Ltd and their authors cannot accept any responsibility for any errors or omissions within this guide, however caused. No responsibility for loss or damage occasioned by any person acting, or refraining from action, as a result of the material in this publication can be accepted by How2become Ltd.

The information within this guide does not represent the views of any third party service or organisation.

CONTENTS

PREFACE

This book has been written with the intention to help and advise aspiring solicitors to become a qualified UK solicitor. 'How to become a solicitor' is the ultimate guide which takes you step-by-step through the demanding and complex process of becoming a solicitor. The guide will provide you with all the important information you will need to know. This will include: the role of a solicitor, what it is like to be a solicitor, how to train, educational qualifications, different routes available, career opportunities, and how to be successful within your field.

Since working at How2become, I've found nothing more rewarding than being able to help people enter their chosen career. The opportunity to write this book in conjunction with How2become, has not only been extremely rewarding and enjoyable, but has also provided me with the determination and sheer passion to continue a career in writing.

I have obtained a BA (hons) degree in Media and Cultural Studies, and I fully comprehend the importance of achieving your dream job. Within weeks of leaving university, I started my job at How2become, and it's been the best experience of my life. I left university with the intention of helping others through journalism and writing; and I can proudly say that I have successfully accomplished this goal. Since working at How2become, I have written multiple testing guides and career books, which have proved valuable for hundreds of people who wish to successfully become whatever it is they want to be. It is my absolute pleasure to present you with this book.

This professional guide has been written whilst maintaining a career with the UK's leading career experts. A guide packed full of insightful and detailed information that will help you through the process of becoming a qualified UK solicitor. As you progress through this guide, you will understand the important steps of what it takes to become a successful solicitor.

I have thoroughly enjoyed writing my book, and I hope that it gives you valuable insight into the legal profession. I would like to wish you the very best of luck with all your future endeavours.

ACKNOWLEDGEMENTS

Firstly, I would like to thank all of the incredible and inspiring people I have had the opportunity to work with at How2become. Without the constant support and motivation from my Managing Director, Richard McMunn, and How2become Operations Manager, Joshua Brown, this book would never have happened. I have fundamentally enjoyed being a part of How2become, and I am so grateful for the opportunities and support that they have given me.

Finally, I would like to dedicate and thank my mother Elizabeth, who has always taught me to pursue my dreams, no matter how big or small they are. As she's guided me through my life, she's been my Mum, my rock, my best friend, and without her, I could not have got to where I am today. I am eternally grateful for her endless support, love and willingness to stick by me no matter what. Mum, you are my guidepost for everything.

INTRODUCTION

Welcome, to the ultimate guide to becoming a solicitor. This guide has been designed to help you reach the job of your dreams.

The role of a solicitor has changed quite significantly over the years, but ultimately remains a job that requires a high level of professionalism, skill and commitment. As a result, choosing a career path within the legal world has to be the right decision; not the right decision because someone said so, but the right decision for you. This book will provide you with all the necessary information you will need to consider to make that decision, and understand whether or not a job as a solicitor is rightly for you.

The job role of a solicitor comes with a difficult selection process. This guide will deliver valuable information that will allow you to take your first steps in a long, stressful and competitive journey. If you want to become a solicitor, then you will need to understand the expectations and demanding nature of the profession. The selection process requires hard work, motivation and passion. You need to be fully prepared and fully committed if you want to make it as a successful solicitor. The important thing to ask yourself is 'whether this chosen career is truly for you and whether you are able to embark on this difficult, yet rewarding journey'. This guide will walk you through step-by-step, the process of qualifying to become a solicitor.

Not only does this book give you an insight into the process of becoming a solicitor, it also provides you with valuable guidance and advice to help you land your dream job. As a solicitor, you face the prospect of a challenging yet rewarding career, which offers legal help to people in a whole range of areas. There are many different options to choose from, in regards to which area of soliciting you will enter, so it is important to have as much information as possible, so you can make the right decision.

Foremost, you need to make sure that you are right for the profession, and that more importantly, the profession is right for you. Choosing a career path is one of the biggest and most important decisions a person can make, and so you need to put a lot of time, effort and thought in making the right choices.

This guide will:

- Help you decide whether you are right for the job and whether the job is right for you.

- Understand the important stages of the selection process and what is expected.

- Give you a step-by-step guide through the application process and everything you need to know in terms of education, skills, qualifications and experience.

- Give you an insight into what employers are looking for in terms of potential employees and the opportunities available.

- Guide you through the interview stages and the typical questions you are likely to be asked.

- Provide tips and advice throughout, to help you on your journey of becoming a solicitor.

This guide primarily focuses on providing valuable information so that you can make informed decisions regarding the choices available. Taking the first steps into your future as a solicitor starts right here. Take your time, and read through this guide carefully to ensure that you are fully prepared for what is to come.

Remember, work hard, believe in yourself, and success will come your way.

CHAPTER 1

THE SOLICITOR

The legal profession is made up of many different types of people. From lawyers to magistrates, judges to solicitors; they all serve within the legal sector, and practice law in different ways.

Now, it may seem like an obvious answer, but it is important to understand what we actually mean when we say 'solicitor', and how this is different to other legal jobs. All legal professionals deal with the law in different ways, and play a different role in the process of legal duties.

How exactly do solicitors differ from magistrates? How do I know whether to become a solicitor or a barrister? What position would suit me best? All these questions are commonly asked amongst aspiring solicitors. It is imperative that you understand where your strengths lie and where you see yourself in terms of your legal career.

IMPORTANT TIP

Make sure you understand the difference between a solicitor and a barrister. You need to comprehend where your strengths and weaknesses lie in order to work out where you would best fit within the legal sector.

What is a solicitor?

A solicitor is a 'type' of lawyer; a licensed legal practitioner who provides a legal service for society. The important thing to remember is to distinguish the difference between a solicitor and a barrister. A barrister does not play a role in litigation, but instead provides legal advice. Barristers usually do not work face-to-face with the clients; they only become involved in a case when a solicitor requests them to speak on the behalf of their client.

A solicitor, on the other hand, takes instructions from clients and advise them on necessary courses of legal action. To define the role of a solicitor more definitively; the Oxford Dictionary states that a solicitor is:

"A member of the legal profession qualified to deal with conveyancing, the drawing up of wills, and other legal matters. A solicitor may also instruct barristers and represent clients in some courts" (Oxford Dictionary, 2015).

A solicitor is a legal practitioner who primarily deals with legal issues before they are taken to court. Their job is to first and foremost, offer legal aid and advice to their clients, and provide reasoning and solutions when required to do so.

The role of a solicitor

The role of a solicitor is to work directly with the client to ensure a rapport is built, and understand the client's needs, goals, ambitions and requirements, in order to provide a solid basis for resolution. A solicitor needs to be vigilant in deciding what the best course of legal action is, and how they can help their clients in the best possible way.

A solicitor deals with the preparation of legal documentations and conducts legal support outside of the courts. They may also use their time to represent clients who are not able to afford legal services, also known as 'pro bono' (see Chapter 8).

Once a solicitor is qualified, the role differs depending on a number of things. Solicitors can choose to work in private practises, in-house for commercial or industrial organisations, local or national governments or service in the courts. The role of a solicitor will ultimately depend on the area of specialism, and the nature of the case. However, typical duties can include:

- Meeting and interviewing existing and potential clients.
- Taking clients instructions.
- Advising clients on the law and the best legal action to take.
- Drafting documentations, letters, emails and contracts tailored

specifically to the needs of the client.

- Researching and analysing previous legal issues which could implement the case that is being worked on.
- Acting on behalf of clients.
- Negotiating with opposing parties.
- Instructing barristers when required.
- Preparing papers for court cases.
- Keeping up-to-date with the changes and developments of the legal sector, including reading up on previous cases in journals and reports.
- Continuing the professional development (CPD), required by all solicitors.

It would be your job to provide answers and resolutions for paying clients, and therefore it is imperative that you are able to show high levels of skills, knowledge and determination.

The History of the Role

The role of a solicitor has changed considerably over the years. Within the legal profession over the last three decades, through steadily rising profits, revenues, headcounts and increased salaries, the legal industry has had to adapt its infrastructure and ideas in relation to contemporary values. Factors such as the recession, and a lack of job opportunities, have forced the legal industry to change the way in which they conduct their services, in order to remain relevant. Without adapting to the needs of society and the environmental changes which we as a society have faced in the last ten years, the legal sector would simply not work. The legal system has to remain a strong, relevant and influential service; its conditions, processes and services have to also remain strong, relevant and up-to-date to result in an effective and competent service.

It is clear that a life in the legal profession requires the ability to undergo strong changes. Solicitors need to be constantly aware and open to the fact that their careers can change on a day-to-day basis.

Solicitors need to make sure that the advice they are giving is correct and reliable, and ensure a service that people are confident in.

Becoming a solicitor can be complex, stressful and overwhelming, but the rewards and opportunities are lucrative. The rest of this chapter will focus on the key areas which you should take into account when making your final decision on whether or not the role is right for you.

Opportunities for Progression

The ultimate goal for any solicitor is to move up the ranks and become a partner in a private practice. Partnerships are owned and managed by the partners. If you are a salaried partner, you will have a similar status to equity partners, but will not have a share in the profits of the firm. It can take eight or more years to become a partner in a large firm, and possibly five years to become a partner in a smaller firm. How long it takes you to reach your goal of becoming a partner in a law firm really does depend on your knowledge, ability and drive.

Working Hours

You need to remember that working as a solicitor is extremely demanding, and will take up large amounts of your time. Do not expect to enter this role as a 9 to 5 job; this is highly unlikely. The working hours will vary according to different departments within the law firm, and how busy you are.

During busy periods, you can expect to work a 12-hour day. This is not uncommon amongst law firms. These may involve early morning starts, late finishes and weekend work. Thus, you need to make sure that you are 100% committed to the job and understand the expectations of the role.

As a solicitor, you will often find that your job is unpredictable. You may find yourself cancelling plans at short notice; you may find yourself working from early morning until late evening. The hours you work will also depend on your level within the firm. If you are a trainee, you are probably less likely to experience these severe long hours, whereas a senior solicitor or a partner in a law firm will be expected to put in the extra hours when required.

Expected Salary and Conditions

Salaries for qualified solicitors can range from £25,000 to £75,000, and partners in large firms or the heads of in-house legal departments, can expect to make in excess of £100,000.

Salaries of solicitors at the senior level or who have great experience will vary considerably depending on the size and location of the firm they work for, recent performance, the area for which they practice, and the level of seniority the solicitor has achieved.

Ultimately, your salary should increase with time. As your experience and skills are put into action, and you spend the time working on bettering your performance, the more likely you are to see that increase.

Below, is a table to indicate an approximate salary in terms of what you can expect, and the minimum salary authorised by the Solicitors Regulation Authority.

Trainee Solicitor	SRA Stipulation for Minimum Salary	Recommended Starting Salary
Central London	Formerly £18,590, now no minimum	£19,040
England and Wales	Formerly £16,650, now no minimum	£16,940

At the back of this guide, in the 'Helpful Resources' chapter, you will find a list of law firms, what they pay training contracts, and what they pay upon qualifying.

Expenses

Another aspect you should consider is the expenses. Training to be a solicitor is extremely expensive, and therefore you need to be fully committed in pursuing this career and be 100% certain that this is the right career path for you.

As you move forward in your quest to become a solicitor, you must not only consider the cost of the courses you need to take, but other expenses such as:

- Living expenses.
- Travel (to and from campus).
- Study costs such as books, school supplies, possible printing and photocopying.
- Food.
- Social life (cost obviously varies depending on how and where you socialise).

The following information is an approximation of cost per phase of your studies to become a solicitor. Please understand that the numbers listed are averages and/or trending numbers and that your individual cost will vary depending on a multitude of variables.

▶ Undergraduate Degree

Since 2012, the government has allowed universities to charge fees of up to £9,000 per annum. Since universities are able to decide how closely they will charge to this maximum, it is best that you check with the individual institutions to see how much they are charging. The majority of universities will indeed exercise their right to charge the maximum fee, of £9,000.

There are two types of student loans available at this stage of your education. The 'Tuition Fee Loan' is a student loan for the full amount of your fees, or £9,000. A student loan for maintenance, often called the 'Living Costs Loan', will vary depending on what city you will be studying in, and whether you live with family or live on your own. For the 2014-2015 academic year, the grant for living alone and studying in London was £7,751.

Generally speaking, many students will need to borrow both. These loans are repayable after graduation, whereby you will be expected to pay 9% on any earnings that are above the repayment threshold. The threshold is currently set at £21,000.

A number of grants are also available through your university, or indirectly when you utilise the normal loans application process. This money comes from your local education authority. Maintenance grants are based on your earnings or the earnings of your parents. If awarded a maintenance grant, it could be up to £3,387 per year. Grants are different from loans in the fact that they do not have to be paid back.

▶ Postgraduate Courses

If you did not get a degree in law, you will need to study the GDL. For a full-time course in London, this cost is currently £9,820 for the 2013-14 academic year. Take note that this cost does not include your living costs.

If you are studying the LPC, a full-time course in London for the 2014-15 academic year will cost £14,750. Again, this does not include your living costs.

Neither the LPC nor the GDL are funded under normal grant or student finance arrangements, because they are not usually eligible for local education authority funding. However, there are times when funds are available, but it will depend on your personal circumstances. It will be up to you, in those instances, to contact your local education authority to obtain more information in order to see if you qualify.

▶ Bank Loans and Sponsorship

Funding for your GDL and/or the LPC is normally done by getting a high-street bank loan. Many banks see you as a good investment due to the fact that you will be a professional, and therefore are more likely to be earning enough money to repay the loan. Unlike government student loans, a bank loan will need to be paid as soon as the course is over, no matter what you earn.

If you do your GDL or the LPC at BPP Law School, and hold a UK passport, you are offered the possibility of 'The Law Loan' from Investec Bank. This will allow you to take out a loan to cover the cost of multiple courses. This loan is for up to £25,000.

Occasionally City, international or large regional law firms will provide sponsorship for the GDL and/or LPC for those students that they have already selected for a training contract. Rarely will other bodies offer sponsorship for their trainees. Some will offer limited financial help. If you have been recruited during your education and the firm offers to sponsor you through your postgraduate courses, they will generally choose a provider that will offer certain modules. These modules will be tailored to the firm's practice.

CHAPTER 2

THE ROLE STRUCTURE

As a solicitor, you will need to understand the different roles each person plays within the legal sector. Each position along the chain, holds different levels of responsibility and expectations, and this will vary depending on where you are in terms of your career.

The Associates Life

Once you qualify and secure employment, you will most likely become an "assistant" or "associate" solicitor. Simply stated, you are considered an employee of the firm, and will most likely be working under the supervision of a senior associate or partner, making a fixed salary.

Depending on what type of firm you work with, the areas of work in which you practise, the partners that supervise you, and your experience; your duties will vary. Generally speaking, you will need to work hard, taking responsibility for your own clients without the need of regular supervision.

THE ASSOCIATES LIFE
A qualified and employed solicitor. Usually considered as an 'assistant', this role will allow you to put into action all of the skills, knowledge and formal training you have gained.

Gradually, associates of a law firm are able to take on more responsibility as they progress. You will deal with your own clientele base, whist still being guided by the partner or supervisor of that law firm.

Associates can become senior associates, then salaried partners and then full-equity partners. This is a great starting point for any solicitor who is serious about progressing in their career.

Partnership

Partnership is the ultimate goal for almost every solicitor. Law firms are based on partnerships; they are owned and managed by partners of the firm. You can become a full partner, in which you own a portion of the firm and share in the profits, or you can become a salaried partner where you do not share in the profits.

How long it will take you to become a partner of a law firm will depend on your work ethic, and the firm in which you work. In general, you can expect it to take eight or more years of post-qualifying to gain a partnership with a large commercial firm, and possibly around five years at a smaller, less commercial firm. Ultimately, how fast you progress will depend solely on your determination and desire to do well within the legal sector.

Ultimately, much will depend solely on you and your determination, experience and skill to do well within the legal sector.

It is generally the goal of a newly qualified solicitor to eventually become a partner in their dream law firm. Don't let your focus on that goal cloud your experience. If you work hard and do your job well, your goal will be fulfilled sooner than you think.

Continuing Your Professional Development (CPD)

Take note, that no matter what stage you are at within your legal career, and however far up you are on the career ladder, you will still be expected to take a course in continuing your professional development (CPD).

All solicitors are required by The Solicitors Regulation Authority (SRA) to update their knowledge and skills on an annual basis.

This is fundamental to your training, and will ensure you remain competent at your job.

When your training contract ends, your formally assessed training does not. Under the continuing professional development (CPD) programme, newly qualified solicitors (NQs) must complete one hour of continuous training each month of their first year. After that, solicitors must take 16 hours of continuing educational courses per year.

There are many ways to earn CPD credit, including:

- Researching
- Mentoring
- Writing on law
- Attending Law Society-accredited courses.

Every solicitor must take Stage One of the SRA management course to fulfil their CPD requirement. Solicitors are required to attend a course in Management and this comprises of 7 hours attendance in at least three of the following areas:

- Managing finance
- Managing the firm
- Managing client relations
- Managing information
- Managing people

Fundamentally, continuing your professional development requires you to meet the standard requirements of the CPD scheme. Your participation in the CPD allows you to enhance your credibility and knowledge, which ultimately allows you to remain commercially competitive.

CHAPTER 3

THE STRUCTURE OF THE LEGAL INDUSTRY

Before I talk you through the step-by-step process of how to become a solicitor, first, you should have a strong understanding of the legal industry, specifically in terms of how it is structured, and what you can work towards.

There are several legal matters that require the assistance of solicitors. Solicitors use their expertise in regards to a whole range of legal matters. The types of client you will have to deal with, and the issues you will face, will depend on the area you wish to specialise in. The more you know about becoming a solicitor, the more likely you are to make an informed decision in regards to where you see yourself in terms of your career.

It is not uncommon for solicitors to start out in one area of practice and end up in another area of practice. Many areas of law overlap and so it is actually a great idea to become proficient in more than one type of law.

Types of Law Firms

When deciding upon your course of study, creating your CV, interviewing, and eventually practising law; you need to consider what type of law firm you want to work for.

Here is a broad set of categories that can help you to establish which type of firm might best match the goals you have for your career and your working style:

- **General practice, legal aid and advice centres:** It is predicted that thousands of small partnerships and individual practitioners will ultimately wind up giving way to larger franchises and alternative business structures.

- **International firms:** Located mostly in the City of London, these firms can contain a couple of offices or a global network.

- **National/regional firms:** These firms are located in London, Birmingham, Liverpool, Manchester, Bristol, Leeds, Nottingham, Cardiff, and Newcastle.

- **UK-focused City firms:** These firms usually offer broad commercial training. They usually specialise in one or two areas. Some may also have a private client practice and longstanding relationships with wealthy individuals and trusts.

As an aspiring solicitor, you will need to understand the different areas of practise that you can work in. You will need to be able to provide expert knowledge, expertise and assistance in a range of situations.

Areas of Practise

Typical areas that you may wish to specialise can be categorised under the following headings:

- **Commercial issues** - Issues related to businesses. Settling disputes, helping new companies get started, serving as an advisor for complex and corporate transactions.

- **Personal issues** - Issues such as divorce, family disputes, quarrels concerning children, buying or selling properties, wills, criminal litigation.

- **Private and Public disagreements** - Protecting the rights of individuals who may have been unfairly treated or injured, and ensuring that they are rightly and properly compensated.

Administrative & Public Law	Technology, Media & telecommunications	Sports	Agriculture & Rural Issues	Aviation and Aerospace
Advertising & Marketing	Defamation/ Reputation Management	Fraud	Professional Discipline	Banking & Finance
Personal Injury	Corporate Finance/Mergers & Acquisitions	Charities	Shipping & Trade	Dispute Resolution
Intellectual Property	Employment, Pensions & Incentives	Clinical Law	Construction & Engineering	Environment
Capital Markets	Commercial Property and Real Estate	Life Sciences	Professional Negligence	Corporate Tax
Housing/ Tenant & Landlord	Energy & Natural Resources	Immigration	Competition & EU Law	Financial Services
Insolvency & Restructure	Projects/Project Finance	Outsourcing	Crime	Crime Insurance & Reinsurance
Company & Commercial	Civil Liberties & Human Rights	Private Client	Family & Matrimonial	Media & Entertainment

If someone were to say to you, "I am a lawyer"; this could mean many different things. Lawyers specify in certain legal matters, so it is important to fully comprehend what type of practise you want to work in. Fundamentally, each type of lawyer is like a completely different job altogether.

Each discipline and/or type of practise has its own demands. Every soliciting job, no matter whether you work for a corporate company, or deal with individuals, requires a whole different mind-set. Knowledge, temperament, relationships; all differ depending on the type of practise you choose to work for.

The following pages will indicate different profiles of individual solicitors who specialise in an array of areas. You need to have a strong understanding of the type of firm that will suit both your desired career path, and professional expectations.

Types of Practice

So, to get an idea of what each area of practice entails, I have provided you with the following general descriptions of the types of practice you can get into. Whilst some areas of practice may have many more sub-areas than others; the descriptions will give you a basic idea of what may be involved.

Administrative & Public Law – This area of law provides services for a range of topics; from solar energy tariffs, to the right to die. Also covered, would be areas such as the treatment of a disabled person by a local authority, or a child's right to an education. Some firms advise local authorities or central government departments in areas of energy, transport and waste disposal.

Advertising & Marketing – This area of law advises advertising agencies during instances of defamation or infringement of third-party IP rights. Also, copy clearance advice is also given. Other solicitors in this area of practice may give advice on contracts with big-brand clients and celebrities who appear in their clients' commercials.

Agriculture & Rural Issues – Clients in this area of law would be landowners and rural businesses, stables, farmers, large dairies, feed manufacturers, farmers' co-operatives, insurers and banks. Advice in relation to wills, trusts and partnership law, as well as agricultural tenancies and other types of property law would also be common practice.

Aviation & Aerospace – This type of solicitor would provide regulatory, insurance and commercial advice and litigation services to the world's airlines, manufacturers and financiers. Aircraft finance and leasing are key areas of activity. Other issues that may be covered by this solicitor would include competition and state aid, emissions trading rules, insolvency, restructuring, and aviation disasters.

Banking & Finance – A solicitor in this area of practice may act for the banks, carrying out due diligence on project contracts, as well as structuring and formulating security packages. Some may advise borrowers themselves, or act for companies and sponsors that want to borrow from a bank to fund an infrastructure project. Common tasks would be reviewing contracts and drafting and negotiating contracts.

Capital Markets – Capital markets solicitors will work primarily with transactions involving debt or equity securities for the public or a group of investors. They conduct due diligence review on the issuer of the securities, draft the prospectus and other disclosure documents, negotiate agreements between the issuer and its advisers and navigate the transaction through regulatory hurdles.

Charities – These solicitors will advise the not-for-profit and social enterprise sector. Wills and trusts to real estate and commercial law are grounds that would be covered by charities solicitors. Some will specialise in the creation and governance of registered charities and others will specialise in litigation over disputed legacies. Real estate, trusts and wills are also a commonly covered area within this spectrum.

Civil Liberties & Human Rights – A major area of this type of practice includes extradition law.

Clinical Law – Clinical negligence lawyers advise in relation to injury or death coming from inadequate or incorrect medical treatment or diagnosis. Some represent the claimants and others represent the defendants.

Commercial Property & Real Estate – These solicitors act for a variety of clients; including investors, developers, landowners, public sector bodies and governments. They will focus on buying, selling, letting and developing land. Planning, construction, litigation, environmental and tax law will commonly run side-by-side with real estate law. This area of law can operate across sectors such as corporate, investment, banking, health, education, insolvency, charities, agriculture and private wealth.

Company & Commercial – Two areas of work for this type of solicitor are contentious or non-contentious. Contentious work includes litigation and arbitration for disputes that come from a range of commercial, corporate and other transactions. Commercial solicitors will also advise on operation and termination of agreements and the negotiation and/or settlement of disputes before proceedings are commenced. Non-contentious work includes joint venture and project development agreements, outsourcing and advertising, logistics and manufacture arrangements.

Competition & EU Law – Merger control, regulatory, court proceedings as well as sector-specific regulation, public sector, state aid and utility procurement issues.

Construction & Engineering – Clients for this area include insurers, architects, industry associates, public authorities, governmental bodies for major corporations and partnerships and contractors. Work may include resolution of disputes by litigation, adjudication, mediation or arbitration. Drafting and negotiating contracts, advising on projects, health and safety, insurance, insolvency and environmental matters are other areas of non-contentious work within this field.

Corporate Finance (Mergers & Acquisitions) – These solicitors advise companies on all aspects of buying and selling whole businesses or business assets.

Corporate Tax – A corporate tax solicitor will advise on tax-efficient means of selling, acquiring or restructuring assets, documenting and negotiating transactions, and ensuring the smooth completion of deals. Contentious tasks would be advising on tax litigation and investigation, conduct litigation in civil court and negotiations with tax authorities.

Crime – Criminal solicitors deal with all aspects of the criminal justice system, from initial police interviews all the way up to the courtroom trial. They deal with the full spectrum of offences, from murder all the way down to minor motoring misdemeanors. Criminal solicitors will advise both the accused and the prosecution.

Defamation/Reputation Management – This area generally has two types of clients, the media and the rich or famous. Libel and privacy are two major areas this type of solicitor will deal with.

Dispute Resolution – This area covers both commercial litigation and arbitration. Arbitration offers a way for parties to resolve their commercial disputes in a private forum, whereas commercial litigation involves the resolution of disputes in the corporate and commercial sphere.

Employment, Pensions & Incentives – Employment solicitors handle all areas of employment law. This would include workplace monitoring, staff restructuring, discrimination and whistle-blowing.

Energy & Natural Resources – This area of law covers nuclear and renewable, pipelines, refineries, oil and gas projects, and liquefied natural gas among other things such as bio-fuels, carbon capture and trading. These issues may be domestic or international in scope.

Environment – Environmental solicitors are involved in a wide range of subjects; health and safety, contaminated land, renewable energy, waste, risk management and environmental finance as well as property and commercial transactions, nuclear law and litigation. Clients include community groups, companies of all sizes, individual governments and local authorities.

Family/Matrimonial – These solicitors advise on a wide range of legal issues relating to marriage, civil partnerships and unmarried couples. Separation, divorce, financial claims, pre and post-nuptial/civil partnership agreements and cohabitation. They will also help settle cases that involve children such as contact, support and adoption.

Financial Services – One of the most in-demand areas of law, the focus is on advising about the many regulations in financial services, including capital requirements and the implementation of Base III rules. This solicitor would also be called in to help guide clients through the investigation of reporting failures, money laundering or insider dealing.

Fraud – Solicitors in this field will advise clients on a small scale for credit card skimming all the way up to large scale rogue traders.

Housing (landlord & tenant) – A solicitor that practices housing law will deal with cases ranging from terrorising teens, to bankrupt restaurateurs who owe back rent. They will also deal with unlawful sub-lettings and additions to leased properties, such as a roof extension or a cellar. This area of law focuses a lot on the statutory obligations of public authorities to the poor or homeless.

Immigration – This area of practice deals with matters of immigration and nationality. Asylum, human rights, and immigration status for employees are all areas an immigration solicitor would be dealing with.

Insolvency (restructuring) – An insolvency solicitor would be called when a company or organisation cannot pay their debts any longer and faces liquidation. These solicitors also advise organisations on how to avoid such situations and create contingency plans in case the worst happens.

Insurance (reinsurance) – These solicitors are responsible for advising their clients on investment management, coverage disputes, mergers and acquisitions of insurers, documentation, and the transfer of books and business between insurers.

Intellectual Property – Solicitors in this practice advise in two main areas: 'Hard' which relates to patents, registered designs and registered trademarks, and 'Soft' which relates to unregistered trademarks, database rights, trade secrets, copyright, unregistered design rights, confidential information and passing off.

Life Sciences – These solicitors practice in the healthcare sector, including advising on patents for new drugs and patient litigation to protect existing rights. Also included in this practice would be regulatory advice on matters such as accurate labelling and marketing of drugs to competition law issues.

Media & Entertainment – Clients in this area of practice include performers, managers, agents, owners of festival grounds and theatres, publishers, broadcasters, advertising agencies, distributors and big brands who employ celebrities to endorse their products.

Outsourcing – These solicitors are responsible for drafting the agreements for outsourcing arrangements. These agreements are very vast and complex, and when the contract isn't followed it is up to the litigator to clean up the mess.

Personal Injury – This area of law falls under the Law of Tort. This involves civil law cases to obtain compensation for sustained injuries and to put the injured person back into the position they would have been in if they had not been injured. This can involve high-profile disaster cases through traffic accidents and health and safety cases.

Private Client – This type of solicitor generally looks after the affairs of an individual client or clients. They will plan and manage all aspects of the individuals finance, including onshore and offshore trusts, wills and probate, and tax matters. They will also handle a lot of charity work and advise on specific legal issues, such as commercial and property matters that affect charitable organisations.

Professional Discipline – Clients that can be represented by a professional discipline solicitor would be dentists, nurses, doctors, lawyers, teachers, social workers and police officers. They will deal with issues such as fraud, inappropriate sexual relationships and assault.

Professional Negligence – Even solicitors and barristers may be represented by this type of solicitor. Any professional that gives negligent advice, gross miscalculations or bad recommendations, will be represented by this type of solicitor.

Projects (project finance) – A project solicitor would be used when legal advice is needed for a large project. For example, the constructions of a new hospital, or a large wind farm, are both areas that a project lawyer would oversee.

Shipping & Trade – Areas of practice within the shipping & trade section such as transport collisions, lending and security, charters and shipbuilding contracts.

Sports – This area involves legal issues in the world of both amateur and professional sports. It will overlap with employment law, contract law, competition law and tort, as well as intellectual property, privacy and defamation.

Technology, Media & Telecommunications – Solicitors practicing in this area of law advice on commercial and technical issues, regulatory changes, market developments, and legislation.

Having an understanding of the area in which you want to work, will ultimately put you ahead of others who are unsure of where they see themselves in terms of their legal career.

Now that you have a broader understanding of the types of practise and areas in which you can specify, you need to ask yourself, "is the job of a solicitor right for me?"

Within the next chapter, you will be able to see what life is like through the eyes of a qualified solicitor. I conducted an interview with a qualified corporate lawyer, who is also a partner in a law firm. I have provided this insightful interview in hope to answer some of the typical questions you may have in regards to a career in the legal sector.

CHAPTER 4

IN THE EYES OF A SOLICITOR

Case Study "In the eyes of a solicitor" – a qualitative study into the business and development of lawyers.

Within this chapter, I have provided you with an extensive one-to-one interview with a qualified solicitor.

The purpose of this interview is to act as a 'frequently asked questions' section, which will hopefully answer some of the most important questions people have in regards to becoming a solicitor.

Interview

In your own words, how would you define your role as a solicitor?

My job is, amongst other things, to sit down with the client, get to know the client, understand what the client's goals are, what their fears are, and then what their ambitions are for them personally, their family and their business. Only when we have done that can we help them get to where they want to be.

How do you become a solicitor?

The quickest route is, you go to university and do a law degree, then you go to law school to do the LPC (legal practice course), and after that, you do a training contract with a law firm. A training contract generally lasts for two years. In my firm, people spend four months in six seats/departments over two years.

If you haven't done a law degree, can you still become a solicitor?

You are able to do a conversion to law, so you do two years of law school. You do the GDL (graduate diploma in law) in the first year, followed by the LPC in the second, and then go on to do the training contract.

Why did you want to become a solicitor?

Probably because my dad wanted me to, initially! I did a 4 year law degree (including a year abroad), but it wasn't really until the last two years of my degree that I decided that I wanted to become a lawyer. I then went on to do the LPC and was fortunate enough to get a training contract with a good commercial firm.

Do you like the position you are in, in terms of your career?

Doing what I do (commercial law), in the team that I do it in, suits me as a person. I think other areas of law probably wouldn't have suited me. I was fortunate that when I did my rotation, I managed to sit in the corporate team and the rest is history.

What do you need in order to become a successful lawyer?

The intellectual ability is a key attribute in the making of a successful lawyer. You've got to have the intellect to do the job. You're expected to be pragmatic and sensible in your approach to things. If the client has a problem, you are expected to help them to find the solution with as minimum fuss as possible. There is something called a CPD (continuing professional development) whereby there is a requirement for solicitors to do 16 hours a year of updating, refreshing knowledge and intellectual ability.

Do you think the legal sector has changed over the years?

The job of a lawyer has changed fundamentally since I qualified in 2001. You're not just expected to be a lawyer sitting at your desk waiting for the work to roll in. You have to go out and market, network and develop contacts to increase your chances of winning clients and new work. It is the responsibility of the partners in a law firm to get that work in. That work comes from existing clients, new clients, as well as referrals from your network of contacts. A law firm is a business where you have to manage people, market, have knowledge of the finances, win work and deliver that work to the clients.

What do your clients expect?

People nowadays don't want a lawyer who sits on the fence, they want you to actually commit to an answer, to give meaningful and practical advice. So you also have to be commercially aware, able to look at the law and consider it in the context of what the client wants to achieve, which is why you spend time with the client at the beginning to understand what they want and why they want to do it. You then use your experience in practice to help them to get there.

What does your average working day consist of?

It really varies. The last three weeks I've barely been at my desk. A combination of work, business development, meetings and training. Days frequently involve all of that to a greater or lesser degree. The work you do in a law firm also depends on your level of qualification and seniority. Junior lawyers will spend more time in the office because at the beginning of their careers, the emphasis has to be on becoming good lawyers, improving their knowledge base and obviously as they become more senior and grow, they will gain more responsibilities, as more is expected of them.

What particular skills does a firm look for in a potential candidate?

Different firms look for different things. The job market is very competitive. It's really important to try and match the right firm with the right people. People will be more likely to have a successful application if they are applying to a firm where they feel that their values are aligned. Every firm has its own ethos and approach. We look for hard working people, who have common sense and commercial awareness, and at the same time, who like to have fun. We recruit trainees with the intention that they develop their career in the firm after they qualify.

Is there particular funding/sponsorship for your studies?

It's expensive, because you've got to be able to pay for the university tuition fees and law school fees. If you do a 3 year degree at £9,000 of tuition fees a year, and do the LPC, that alone can be in excess of over £30,000 plus living costs. If you're lucky, you might get a training contract with a firm that provides some assistance with your law school fees, which can be anything from a loan or in some cases, they pay off some or all of it. It is really important that people understand what they are getting into and every year I go and do a talk at my old university about becoming a solicitor and the pros and cons of it. Really, what people need to understand is that while the first year of your degree at some universities does not count towards your degree result, it does count towards your job applications. People have to make sure that they do everything they can to get as good a grade as possible every year. The firms offering financial support will have the luxury of choosing the best candidates, so candidates with weaker results are less likely to secure training contracts with firms that will provide financial assistance. That's a lot of debt to be taking on.

What would you say is an important attribute for a potential trainee solicitor?

An eye for detail and a common sense approach to things. You wouldn't believe how many training contract applications contain typos!

Are you where you want to be in terms of your career?

I've been very fortunate, as I'm a partner in a top law firm, doing the work I want to do, as part of a great team. It is hugely valuable if you really enjoy the job that you do, as it will show! Clients and colleagues will feed off that.

What would you say the starting point is for any potential trainee solicitor?

They need to take care of the academics so they need to maximise their grades (GCSE/A-Levels/International/Baccalaureate degree). They also need to try and understand what the profession is about, and for some people it's working out whether you want to be a solicitor or a barrister. The best way of achieving that, and to get yourself noticed, is to try and get work experience and placements. Some people also take part in pro-bono clinics and schemes. It is also important, when researching firms and training contracts, to try and look for firms that match your ethos and outlook on life (including any areas of law where you have a specific interest). You need to tailor your applications to show that not only do you want to do the job, but you want to do it with that firm, or a similar firm. There is also a lot of material online which should help applicants to get a better feel for the profession.

What do law firms look for in trainee solicitors?

In my opinion, I wouldn't want someone who just wanted a training contract with any firm, because it's hard to get one. I want someone who is keen on a training contract with my firm because they want to stay on and develop their career with us. If we are investing in the trainees and committing that time, resource and money necessary to produce good lawyers, we want to hold on to them.

What can trainee solicitors expect to earn?

This varies, but there are minimum requirements imposed by the Law Society in regards to salaries for training contracts. There's a minimum for London and Non-London. So as long as the firm is paying that minimum, it is up to them how much they decide to pay and it can become competitive. Most firms that take on trainees will look to attract good quality applicants by offering salaries significantly over the minimum, as well as the financial support detailed above. When trainees qualify, there is a jump in salary and that jump will depend on the type of firm they work for. Remember though, if you want the very high salaries, you won't be working a 9 to 5 job!

What are the downfalls of becoming a solicitor?

I think sometimes the impact it can have on your personal life in terms of having to cancel plans at very short notice because something crops up and you have to get it resolved at that time. It's not a 9 to 5 job. The days vary. You could start at 8 in the morning and get the train home at 6 in the morning the next day, but that is a rare extreme.

Typical hours for me are usually between 9 and 7. It can be stressful. Clearly at times there are pressure points, but we are there to help clients to achieve their goals, so there is responsibility there. If people are paying money for a service, they quite rightly expect you to provide the best possible service you can offer. Whatever area of law you are in, you ought to care about what you are doing. On the flip side, there are real plusses doing what we do. It is incredibly rewarding for a lawyer when they are a key component in helping the client to achieve its goal, whether that is concluding a transaction, buying their dream house for them or helping them after they have been involved in an accident.

Any other advice you would give for someone who wants to become a solicitor?

Take care of academics. It is incredibly competitive to get a training contract, so some serious self-reflection is required. Sit down and think whether or not you want to be a lawyer, and if so which kind, barrister or solicitor. Then do what you can to get the work experience to try and find the right firm for you. Networking is not just important for the qualified lawyers. As potential applicants, network with the lawyers you meet when they go down to the universities or law fairs. If you impress, they may put in a good word for you!

Ultimately, what would you say the main things a trainee solicitor needs to possess?

Intellectual ability is a given, but we also look for commercial awareness, good people skills and a hard worker. If you put the time and effort in, you will get to where you want to be.

Hopefully, this extensive interview with a qualified solicitor gives you an insight into the legal profession, and makes your decision on whether to pursue the role, a little easier. In the next chapter of this guide, we will look at whether the position is right for you personally, and explore your further options.

CHAPTER 5

IS THE JOB RIGHT FOR ME?

Nobody knows 100% whether a career change is right for them. However, choosing to become a solicitor should be considered extremely carefully. The process of becoming a solicitor demands extremely high levels of commitment and determination, and therefore is not something that should not be entered lightly. This process will likely to occupy you for many years beyond your initial training, so you need to think long and hard before making the decision.

It is imperative that you fully comprehend the requirements and the standards to which you will be held. As a solicitor, you can expect a long-winded process that will require long hours, commitment and ambition to succeed.

This section will demonstrate the important demands and requirements of the job role; and make you question whether this challenge is something you can endure throughout the rest of the training process.

Below you will find a list of personal qualities, which may or may not fit with the profession. Think about your own personality, and how it relates with the issues listed.

If you are normally the type of person to shy away from paperwork and research, this may not be an appropriate position for you.

Nobody ever knows if they are suitable for a particular career. Consider both the pros and cons of becoming a solicitor, and weigh up whether you can see yourself as a solicitor.

Aside from the many demands that are placed on you as a solicitor, you must also think about the amount of schooling and training that is involved, as well as the cost that goes along with that. While being a solicitor is a rewarding career for the right person, it does come at a cost.

A lot of time and thought needs to be put into the process of becoming a solicitor. Knowledge and skill is not everything; you need to demonstrate the sheer passion, motivation and commitment to the job.

If you are considering becoming a solicitor because you feel it would be easy money, you may want to rethink your decision. Being a solicitor comes with a lot of responsibility and the workload can be overwhelming to those who are only in it for the money or the title. While a lot of people find the work to be rewarding, others find the responsibilities to be more than they had bargained for.

Drawbacks of Becoming a Solicitor

Globally, a career as a lawyer is one of the most highly sought after professions. As with any career, you need to take into account both the advantages and disadvantages of becoming a solicitor. That way, you are able to make a more informed decision about the realities and implications of choosing this particular career.

Ask yourself "can you deal with the demanding nature of this job?"

Of course, there are many rewards as working as a lawyer, however attorney work does have its drawbacks which need to be carefully considered.

Below is a list of some of the drawbacks of gaining a career in the legal profession.

- **Long working hours:** 12 hour days are not uncommon, especially during busy periods. Starting early and working late can happen frequently. Weekend hours may be required on occasion and large City firms can work these extended hours on a regular basis. Many solicitors need to be available to their clients around the clock. That means work does not end as soon as you leave the office. The on-going demands of the job require you to put in the extra time and effort. 50 plus hour weeks are not uncommon for lawyers.

• **Lack of work-life balance:** The fact that you are required to take your job home with you, as a matter of speaking, suggests the implications this can have on a person's work-life balance. Many solicitors complain about the difficulties of maintaining a healthy work and social life, and the impact this has on their personal life.

• **Law debt:** the cost of studying and training to become a solicitor is expensive. If you are not fortunate enough to get your tuition and maintenance paid for, you will need to get a loan of some sort. Therefore, once your studies have ended, you will be required to start paying off these loans.

• **Travel:** While the position is mostly office based, you may need to travel to meet clients, attend court, and overnight stays are occasionally necessary. You may also be expected to work overseas, advising local clients on EU law.

• **Stress:** This can be a very stressful position due to the long hours and workload/responsibilities. Lots of deadlines, responsibilities, and client demands all combine to make practising the law a stressful job.

• **Competitive job market:** Increased competitive pressures have forced many lawyers to settle with less than ideal circumstances regarding their career. It is difficult enough to be a successful solicitor, without the added pressure of competing for one job position, which is expected to receive over 20 applications.

- **Poor public image:** "what do you call 10,000 lawyers at the bottom of the sea? A start." This common lawyer joke demonstrates the public perception towards lawyers. Thus, it is hard to be taken seriously in a society that undermines everything you stand for.

- **Constantly changing legal paradigms:** the practice of law is continuously being challenged by other non-law sources. Lawyers no longer have the monopoly in regards to the law. From self-help websites to the internet, legal advice and understanding can be instantly researched online, without the need of lawyers.

Top 10 Reasons to Become a Solicitor

Amongst all the cons of the job, becoming a lawyer has its lucrative moments – and not just in terms of potential earning.

The following 10 reasons have been carefully put together to illustrate all the positives and benefits of becoming a solicitor. These 10 reasons to become a solicitor will allow you to weigh up the advantages and the disadvantages and make an educated decision on whether or not the role of a solicitor is for you.

- **1. Salary** – Starting with the obvious, one of the largest benefits that comes with the job role of being a lawyer is the salary. Few other careers will start you out with a salary comparable to that of a solicitor. Salaries for qualified solicitors can range from anything from £25,000 to £75,000. Workers at a senior, more experienced level can expect to earn considerably higher than this. Moreover, the more work and experience you obtain, the more likely you are to gain an increase in salary. Another key thing to remember in regards to salary is it is dependent on numerous factors. For example, salary is considered on the basis of location, size and nature of the organisation and experience.

- **2. Fulfilment** – As a solicitor, you will get the opportunity to make a difference in the lives of your clients on a daily basis. Not only can you make a difference with your clients, but you have the chance to make a difference in the lives of people everywhere. One case can set the precedence for many future cases, and therefore plays a vital role in the long-term legal process. The attainment, gratification and satisfaction you will gain from this, is one of the biggest bonuses to the career.

- **3. Advancement** – After obtaining your degree and getting your license to practice law, you now have the opportunity to work your way up to the top at a private practice, where you can eventually become a partner in the firm. You will also have the opportunity to possibly become a judge or an educator. Therefore, becoming a solicitor opens up a number of doors for future career options which inspires motivation and ambition for further career options.

- **4. Education** – Even if you don't go back to school for official advanced training, as a solicitor you will constantly be learning. As a trainee solicitor you will have to undergo continuous training whilst working in order to make sure your knowledge is to a high standard. Even long-term solicitors still undergo training. While working on cases, you will be researching past cases as well as learning about obscure laws and differentiating jurisdictions. There will always be learning opportunities for you to engage in, which will allow you to excel and broaden your horizons in terms of valuable knowledge, expertise and experience.

- **5. Variety** – Not only do you have a wide variety of specialised areas of practice to choose from, but your daily tasks will vary from day-to-day. The job offers versatility as your work life will be changing constantly, making each day different.

- **6. Job Security and Growth** – As long as you do your job well and are a good employee of your firm, your job is secure. No matter the state of the economy, people will always need lawyers.

- **7. Knowledge of the Law** – Practicing the law requires intellectual ability. Not only is your knowledge of the law essential to perform your job successfully, but it offers great comfort for clients to know they are in the capable hands of someone who is highly proficient and knowledgeable. Whether creating a will, dealing with a car accident or buying real estate, your knowledge of the law will come in handy. Despite being beneficial for your clients, it also benefits you as a person. Aside from that, you will find that as a solicitor, your friends and family will come to you for advice about legal or business issues.

- **8. Networking** – While working as a solicitor, you will meet people from all walks of life. It is important to be able to engage in social activity and expand your profile. Whether that's interacting with other lawyers, gaining a new clientele base or simply offering your advice to friends and family, you will begin to notice that networking will help you build up a great professional and expanding portfolio of yourself as a qualified solicitor. Being able to network efficiently proves valuable for any business. It is true by saying that the more you network, the more you will become noticed as a successful solicitor. Networking undoubtedly is the single most important marketing strategies for any business. Being able to make that important connection and building mutual relationships puts you one step closer of expanding your sphere of influence as a solicitor.

- **9. Mobility** – Being a solicitor you will have the ability to work as a solicitor anywhere inside your license to work area. You can work in the city at a large firm for years and then decide to become a lawyer in a small, rural area.

* **10. Ability to Run a Business** – After gaining the appropriate experience working at a law firm, you will have the knowledge and the ability to open your own law firm. This allows you flexibility in terms of setting your own hours, taking the cases that you want and find most interesting and will, above all, put money into your own pockets rather than the pockets of the partners who own the law firm that you worked for.

Becoming a solicitor is extremely hard-work and tiring, and this list of benefits demonstrates that if you put in the effort and you do work hard, you will subsequently reap the rewards. Being a solicitor is a job that provides great opportunities for anyone who is serious about progressing within the field.

No one is ever sure about taking that first step out of their comfort zone into the unknown. Take comfort in the fact that many people feel the same way. The uncertainty and the unknown is enough to stop anyone from pursing their dream job. Amidst all the apprehension and uncertainty, no great accomplishment comes from nowhere. It takes a great deal of drive, and determination, and will power to make that all important step into your future, and if you see your future qualifying as a professional solicitor, then taking that first step onto the path of legal aid is surely right for you.

CHAPTER 6

QUALITIES, SKILLS AND POTENTIAL

While learning and knowing the law and how to represent a client is obviously important, there are other skills and competencies that recruiters will be looking for when making the decision of whether or not to make you part of their team.

Since there are many different skills, qualities and abilities that are required to be a great solicitor, each recruiter will be looking for their own set of important traits as they interview prospective candidates.

> Never try to portray yourself as being something other than what you are. Be yourself, but let your future employer know that you can be moulded into the perfect fit for their firm.

The next several pages will talk about the most common skills and competencies recruiters will look for in graduates. You will also receive tips on how to develop these skills and how to demonstrate your abilities.

Keep in mind that these skills should be touched upon when you create your CV, fill out an application or go through the interview process. Recruiters want to see that you hold a skill-set that will be beneficial to the law firm and to those who are already a part of it.

Team Management

It is common for graduates to be hired as trainee managers. Because of this, team management skills are very important. Team management skills enable you to direct a team to do the best that it can do. While leadership is similar to teamwork, it also means taking responsibility for your team and influencing them.

There is a difference between leadership and team management. Leadership means being a good example, deciding where the efforts need to be focused and setting a direction to proceed. Team

Management is more about getting the best out of all members of the team.

There are many ways to develop leadership and team management skills. Holding an officer position in a student society, student union council positions, becoming a sabbatical officer, volunteering with children's groups or becoming an instructor for a children's group are all good ways to gain responsibility for a group of people. Holding these positions and being able to deliver and give the group what they need is excellent experience that can be used on your CV or job application.

Every business likes to employ people who show willingness to make themselves a valuable team member. Being a lawyer requires a great deal of commitment, not just to yourself and your colleagues, but to your clients.

Commercial Awareness

Recruiters and employers expect at least some level of commercial awareness, and the idea of commercial awareness may be different from employer to employer. Simply stated, commercial awareness is knowing how the business works and where it fits in the world. Keeping up with the news for your particular business type will help you to have more awareness.

Commercial Awareness is imperative for every solicitor who wants to be successful. You need to know how the business functions, what you bring to the firm and how to do your job with the most proficiency.

Employers will expect at least:

- An understanding of their business, familiarity with the end product and a grasp of the activities of the organisation.

- An understanding of the marketplace, major competitors and the differences from each other.

If you would like to impress a recruiter, having these will definitely help:

- An understanding of how the major players in your market are performing.

- An understanding what has happened in the company's past.

- The ability to intelligently speculate what may happen in the future.

To help build your commercial awareness, you could subscribe to journals, RSS or Twitter feeds, and industry magazines. If you make the effort in the year before applying to jobs, you should be in a strong position. Reading about the firm you are interested in and finding the same information on some of their competitors will help you to know some of the differences between firms.

When filling out your application, or creating your CV, you do not want to simply say, 'I read the Legal Times.' Obviously, anyone who has gone through the educational process has the ability to read. Recruiters want to see that you are acting upon what you have read. Here is an example of what you might find on a good application/CV.

'I found a couple of people talking about the same phenomenon, so I decided to look into it. Since it seemed relevant and new, I was able to persuade the people behind it to give a presentation to my society.' Acting upon what you read or hear will set you apart from others.

Creativity

Creativity takes innovation, imagination and intuition. While creativity is important, it is equally important to not overwhelm, or underwhelm, the recruiter. Simply copying and pasting information into your CV will be boring and obvious to your recruiter. This will not impress them at all, and in fact, it will deter them from offering you a position. At the same time, singing their praises may come across as being slightly over the top, inappropriate and while it may grab their attention, it may not be the attention you were looking for.

Imagination.
Innovation.
Intuition.
Intellect.

Starting your own society would be a great way to develop your creative skills. It will give you ample opportunity to be creative by having to come up with ways to attract new members, organise events, raise cash and more. You could also try starting a new project at a part-time job or internship. You obviously would need to set this up with the manager and set targets for success. You would need to measure the popularity of the project, and if successful, the manager may implement it full-time.

When trying to show your creativity on your application or CV, it is important to give an example of how your creativity produced a positive result. Simply stating that you got good grades in your elective art classes will not show the recruiter how creative you are. Generally speaking, your actual academic grades will not show off your skills, other than your ability to study. Recruiters want to hear examples of how your ability to creatively think produced something positive.

'When I was challenged with improving our figures, I came up with an idea and after putting together a proposal, I took it to my manager. I was able to persuade her to allow me to run a trial. Since the trial was so successful, my manager added it to our strategy.' This would be an example of how your creativity in the workplace led to a very positive outcome.

Problem Solving

Your ability to problem solve will show your independence. When a recruiter hires you, they want to be sure that you will not come running to the managers or partners every time there is confusion or misunderstanding. It will be up to you to prove that you can take the pressure and take care of any issues properly, on your own.

Using logic and imagination in order to come up with an intelligent solution are skills you will need along with:

> Resilience and level headedness.
> Creativity, logical thinking skills and analytical skills.
> Teamwork skills.

Bransford and Stein created the IDEAL model to help solve problems. This is a great way to process an issue and come up with a solution:

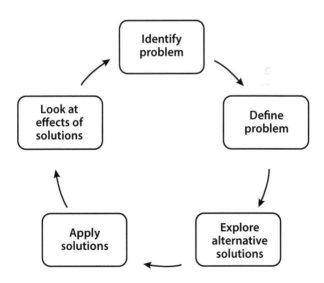

Stage 1 – Identify problem

How do you define a problem? Well, a problem can be defined as "the discrepancy between what we get and what we want". In order to identify the problem, consider the following:

- Identify precisely the difference of what you expected and what you observed.
- A problem needs to be assessed in order to apply a solution.
- A problem needs to be identified in regards to pitfalls, drawbacks and potential consequences.

Stage 2 – Defining the problem

Defining the extent of the problems or any issues that may occur is imperative to providing a solid conclusion.

- You need to find any underlying problem that has occurred or may occur in order to resolve it with effective measurements.

Stage 3 – Explore alternative solutions

It may not be a good idea to base your case on one solution. What if that solution does not work?

- You need to come up with other alternative methods that can be attempted in case one solution does not work.
- You need to establish priorities amongst solutions.
- Remember, what works for one case may not work for another. You are simply working on a hypothesis which may or may not work.

Stage 4 – Apply solutions

As a solicitor, you are expected to provide a solution for your clients. You need to be confident in your abilities to be able to provide an excellent service that generates solutions.

Stage 5 – Look at the effects of solutions

Clients are expecting to see a clear solution to the problems that they were faced with, and as a solicitor it is your job to provide this solution.

- If a problem has been defined, it is probable to achieve the desired level of outcome intended for a client's case.

- The effect of the solution demonstrates how effective your intervention as a solicitor was in the processing of problem solving.

Dealing with everyday life will help you develop your problem solving skills. It is up to you to identify those issues in your daily life and keep track of how you solved those issues. Satisfying a difficult customer, raising enough money to go on a trip, dealing with a computer issue and resolving disputes with a landlord are all ways to develop your problem solving skills.

On your CV or application, use real examples of how you were able to solve a complex problem. Explain the problem you encountered and what ideas you came up with by using the resources that were available to you at that time. Recruiters want to see details. They want to be impressed.

Teamwork

Teamwork is probably the number one attribute recruiters look for when interviewing prospects. Recruiters expect you to show them that you can influence others, collaborate with others and compromise, ignoring your own ego for the better of the team. While you may be the strongest team member, it is important that you still work as a team, encouraging other members to step out of their comfort zone. This is one area where recruiters are not looking for a good leader.

You may already have ample teamwork experience without actually realising it. If you were a member of a sports team, you have experience with teamwork. Another way to gain experience would be to join a quiz team. While you don't want to give the recruiter the idea that you spend all of your time at the pub, the fact that you are on a team where members often compromise what they believe to go along with the rest of the team will let the recruiter know that you are able and willing to be an integral part of their team at the law firm.

When listing your teamwork skills on a job application, CV or during an interview, it is important that you do not take credit for everything you list; saying that you beat the competitor while being part of a team will show the recruiter that you are not actually a team player. It is important that any examples you give show that not only were you a team player, but that you, along with the efforts from everybody else on the team, were able to come up with a group decision that produced a positive outcome.

Time Management is crucial for any successful business. The key tip to remember is to be organised, plan things in advance, and manage yourself and your workload.

'During an Assessment Centre day activity, I was able to help my team to beat another team by encouraging a group atmosphere and supporting the other members of my team. A timid and shy individual on our team had a great solution to the problem, and between myself and the other members of the team, we were able to support her and encourage her to give her answer for the team. Due to us all coming together, her answer won us the competition.' This is a great example of describing your teamwork skills.

Time Management

To effectively manage time, you will need to be able to make judgments about what is important and what is urgent when prioritising your tasks. Also known as 'independent working' and 'self-management', time management is crucial for graduates seeking a position. Oftentimes, while being a solicitor, you will be faced with multiple deadlines at once with the possibility of new work being added to your workload at any time. Knowing how to manage your time effectively will put you one step ahead of your competition.

Developing your time management skills starts while you are in education. If you were able to get through school, study for multiple exams at once, complete papers on time and graduate with great grades, this will be evidence to a recruiter that you have good time management skills. Furthermore, if you have been participating in extracurricular activities and/or part time work while completing your education, this is further evidence that will show you were able to manage your time well.

'While completing my training contract, I was managing multiple projects at the same time. Since each project had a different deadline, I was able to prioritise and divide my time and resources appropriately. I was able to complete all of my projects on time and was given additional projects to work on and complete.' This is an excellent example of how you would explain your time management skills.

Customer Care

Customer satisfaction is important if you want your business to grow. The same principle applies to law firms. Newly graduated solicitors, as a rule, should be giving their clients the same attention and care that they would be giving their boss. You want to help your client make a decision that is right for them. You want to make sure that they feel comfortable and well treated. If this is achieved, they will be more prone to recommend you to someone they know, and continue consultation.

There are three common factors, which stay the same no matter what job you hold within the customer care industry:

- Commercial awareness
- Organisation
- Communication

There are many ways to develop customer care skills. You could work part-time or holiday work in a customer service call centre. Working in the campus library support service, or with IT on campus will also help you gain customer care skills. Really, any job you can find where you have contact with the public will help you build these skills. You might even apply to be a representative at your university. A course rep or halls rep position will allow you to help meet the needs and wants of the student body.

Recruiters want to see that you are comfortable dealing with clients/customers. You must understand that great customer care is not just about making the sale, but making the customer feel comfortable enough to return in the future. If on your application or during an interview you say, *'I had a really annoying customer one time, but I kept my cool and sold them the most expensive product. They probably won't come back, but that's no big deal,'* you will be showing the recruiter that you don't really care about the customer's happiness and the fact that they won't be returning. Instead, show the recruiter that you care about both the client's satisfaction and willingness to return.

Communication

Communication is defined as the effective exchange of information. This is essential when becoming a solicitor. Not only will you have to communicate effectively with your clients, but with your bosses, colleagues, recruiters, professors and any other person who you will encounter on your journey.

Remember, clients come first. Your sole purpose is to provide a service for your clients.

When communicating, presentation skills are important. The way you deliver your message can mean the difference between somebody understanding you or walking away having no clue what you are talking about. Sometimes, less is more when communicating. Too much information can confuse or lose people in the conversation. Knowing who your audience is and tailoring what you say to them will be beneficial.

Gaining communication skills is as easy as putting yourself out there. Go talk to people; introduce yourself and find out more about them. Find a phone job on campus. There are usually a number of jobs like this, ranging from calling alumni for donations all the way to taking calls from students who need some direction. Joining a society will also help you build your communication skills.

When mentioning your communication ability on a job application or with a recruiter in an interview, it is important to effectively communicate your skills with them. If you can't communicate confidently with the recruiter, they will not feel comfortable recommending you for the job. Don't just say, 'I'm a good communicator.' You need to give them examples, demonstrating that your communication skills helped you through a situation.

Essential Skills and Competencies

Aside from all of the skills and qualities that we just talked about, you must be able to show a recruiter that you have all of the basic skills they are looking for. While one firm may expect different abilities than another, all recruiters will expect that you can prove that you have mastered the following skills:

- **Writing** – This skill involves communicating something to a person without having to be there to explain it to the reader. Many people think that by using big words you will sound smarter, but in reality, you want the reader to easily understand what you are trying to convey. This is why many recruiters will expect to see a CV and cover letter. This will show them your skills in effectively bringing across your skills in a clear and easy to read way.

- **Numeracy** – This skill shows your mastery of numbers. Many students stop taking math courses as soon as it is possible. This is fine, but if you are unable to answer a basic math question such as 5 x 9, you will need to brush up on your math skills. Keeping a budget is a perfect way to keep your number skills fresh.

- **Literacy** – This is the skill of reading and comprehension. The first instance in which you will be showing a recruiter your literacy skills will be when you fill out the application for employment. If you are unable to answer the questions on a job application accurately, you will show that your literacy skills are not strong.

- **Presentation** – This skill is most closely linked with communication. By not only verbally presenting something, but visually presenting it as well, if your presentation skills are up to par, the audience will understand what you have presented. Any time you have addressed a group of people, you added to your presentation skills.

- **Organisation** – Any time you take information and/or objects and arrange them in a way that they can be easily found, you are practising your organisational skills. Working a part-time job and completing your studies is an example of how organising your time well becomes a skill. The ability to find all of your research information for multiple subjects, and keep it from getting mixed together is another example of your organisational skills.

- **Stamina** – Resilient is a quality that recruiters are looking for.

Sometimes looking for work after qualifying as a solicitor involves setbacks. Newly qualified solicitors tend to hit a point in their job search when they become fatigued. Keeping at it and not giving up shows a recruiter that your stamina is high. This a valuable asset.

- **Ability to work under pressure** – This skill demonstrates your ability to keep your cool and not become overwhelmed and stressed out during a crisis, or stressful situation. You develop stronger skills in this area when you must study for multiple exams at one time. Taking part in sports teams and other groups in school may also help you develop this skill.

- **Confidence** – This skill is not always an easy one. When meeting with a recruiter, most times you will be nervous, but it is your job to come across as calm and confident. Engaging fully with the employer and keeping upbeat will show them that your confidence is good. Be careful not to exude too much confidence or you will come across as arrogant.

CHAPTER 7

THE ENTRY REQUIREMENTS

Becoming a solicitor is a rewarding yet demanding job that requires a great level of commitment and perseverance. There are a number of different options available. The three main routes which you can take are as formulated below:

The Law Graduate Route

The Non-Law Graduate Route

The Chartered Institute of Legal Executive (CILEx) Route

The key stages of qualifying to become a solicitor in England and Wales is either through the academic route, or the vocational stage.

Whatever route you decide to take, you will be required to undertake the following requirements:

- **Legal Practice Course (LPC)**

- **Period of Recognised Training**

- **Professional Skills Course (PSC)**

QUALIFYING LAW DEGREE
3 years full-time
5 years part-time

Legal Practice Course
1 years full-time
2 years part-time

Period of recognised training
2 years full-time
up to 4 years part-time

NON QUALIFYING LAW DEGREE
3 years full-time
5 years part-time

Common Professional Examination / Graduate Diploma in Law
1 years full-time
2 years part-time

Legal Practice Course
1 years full-time
2 years part-time

CILEx ROUTES
A minimum of 4 GCSEs (including English Language or Literature) or equivalent. Students without formal qualifications may be considered on the basis of experience.

Membership Route
CILEx Level 3 Professional Diploma in Law and Practice
followed by
CILEx Level 6 Professional High Diploma in Law

Membership of CILEx

Fellowship Route
CILEx Level 3 Professional Diploma in Law and Practice
followed by
CILEx Level 6 Professional High Diploma in Law

Fellowship of CILEx
Qualifying employment undertaken

OVERSEAS LAWYERS / QUALIFIED BARRISTERS (QLTS)

Certificate of Eligibility
(issued by the Solicitors Regulation Authority)

Qualified Lawyers Transfer Scheme (QLTS)

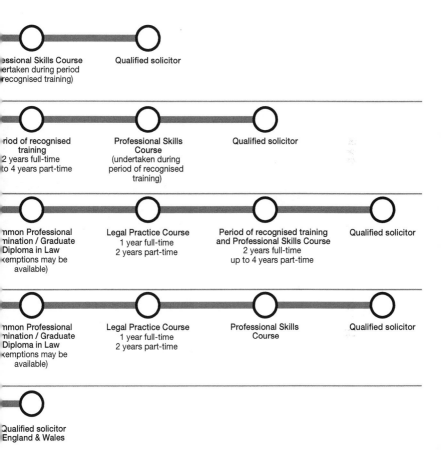

essional Skills Course
ertaken during period
recognised training)

Qualified solicitor

riod of recognised
training
2 years full-time
to 4 years part-time

Professional Skills
Course
(undertaken during
period of recognised
training)

Qualified solicitor

nmon Professional
mination / Graduate
Diploma in Law
xemptions may be
available)

Legal Practice Course
1 year full-time
2 years part-time

Period of recognised training
and Professional Skills Course
2 years full-time
up to 4 years part-time

Qualified solicitor

nmon Professional
mination / Graduate
Diploma in Law
xemptions may be
available)

Legal Practice Course
1 year full-time
2 years part-time

Professional Skills
Course

Qualified solicitor

Qualified solicitor
England & Wales

Take note, there are some important key terms to remember in terms of training and becoming a solicitor. You will be expected to learn and use the key terms listed in the box, throughout your career.

This chapter is broken down into helpful sections, to demonstrate routes that you are able to take in order to become a solicitor, and the training required.

Terms to Remember:

CILEx – Chartered Institute of Legal Executives
CPE – Common Professional Examination
GDL – Graduate Diploma in Law
LPC – Legal Practice Course
PSC – Professional Skills Course

THE
LAW GRADUATE ROUTE

Qualifying with a law degree is probably the most straightforward way to become a solicitor, and the majority of aspiring solicitors opt for this route. Your studies will include all the required aspects of your academic training; essential for any future lawyer.

The key stages of this route include:

Degree in law – 3 years full time.

Legal Practice Course (LPC) – 1 year full time course.

Period of Recognised Training incorporating the Professional Skills Course – 2 years full time.

Admission onto the Roll of Solicitors.

In order to qualify as a solicitor, all these stages (as mentioned above) need to be completed. You will not be able to move forward in your training if you haven't completed a part of the training process.

Stage 1 – Degree in Law

The competition for studying on a law degree programme is fierce. There are many other people, just like you, that are hoping to succeed and become a solicitor. Thus, you are all fighting for that chance to enter the legal sector and become a qualified solicitor.

Please note:
Not all law degrees act as a qualifying law degree. You need to ensure that the university course you undertake is a qualifying law degree.

Exempting law degrees

Some teaching institutions offer shorter law degrees, or a combined degree and a Legal Practice Course. This is known as exempting law degrees. Exempting law degrees combine both the academic and vocational stages to qualify to become a solicitor. Typically, this type of degree usually occurs over a 4 year period, and once completed, you can begin to start your training.

Take care of your academics

Your academic record will need to be very strong, and you will need at least three good passes in any academic A level subjects in order to be accepted into some of the universities.

There are also three ways you can study for your law degree:

- Full-time study through UCAS (offers a searchable database of courses offered by higher education institutions along with details about entrance requirements and information about the universities and colleges).
- Part-time study (you apply directly to the institution of your choice – SRA has a list of institutions which allow part-time studies).
- Long- distance learning.

If you choose to qualify with a law degree, it must be completed within one year of the normal period for a full-time study programme, and within two years of the normal period for a part-time study programme. In order to enter the vocational stage of your training, you must obtain a pass mark of 40% in each subject, no matter the pass mark set by the institution you belong to. The foundation subjects that you will be expected to take at university include:

- Law of the European Union
- Obligations including contract, restitution and tort
- Equity and the law of trusts
- Criminal law
- Property law
- Public law (constitutional law, human rights law and administrative law)

Along with the above subjects, you will also be expected to have the appropriate expertise in the English legal system and legal research.

Once you receive your degree, the next step would be to enrol as a student within the Solicitors Regulation Authority. This will allow you to obtain a certificate of completion, for the academic stage of training. It is after this step that you may then progress to the vocational stage of training.

Stage 2 – Vocational Stage – Legal Practice Course

The vocational stage includes the Legal Practice Course and the training contract. Details of the Legal Practice Course and the training contract can be found further on in this chapter.

Stage 3 – Period of Recognised Training

The next step to qualify as a solicitor, via taking a law degree, is to undertake a period of recognised training. This is usually performed over 2 years and can either be taken whilst completing the vocational LPC stage, or after.

The period of recognised training will enable you to not only put your skills and knowledge to practice, but also gain further experience to help you later on in your career.

Stage 4 – Professional Skills Course (PSC)

This is usually taken when a trainee is undertaking their period of recognised training. It builds on the knowledge and skills that have been acquired throughout the training process of becoming a solicitor. The Professional Skills Course consists of electives and three core compulsory areas:

- Financial and Business skills
- Advocacy and Communication skills
- Client Care and Professional standards

The compulsory elements involve 48 hours tuition, including assessments, and the electives comprise of 24 hours of tuition.

Stage 5 – Admission onto the Roll

Once you have successfully completed all the stages of the law degree route, you can then apply onto the Roll of Solicitors in England and Wales. This entails you to practise as a qualified solicitor.

The Law Degree qualifying Route – Checklist

First year of university

- The first year of university does not count towards your degree. However, when it comes to the time of choosing your second and third year options, make sure you choose subjects that cover the foundation subjects that are required for qualifying solicitors.

- Take the time to talk to lectures and career advisors. You will be able to get information regarding your choices and ideas about your career path.

- Make sure you attend career fairs, open days and research work experience placements – this will ensure that you are one step ahead of your competition.

- Now is the time to research about vacation schemes, work placements and other ways of volunteering.

Second and Third year

- Make use of the careers specialists on site. They are there to guide you through the process, and help you make the right decisions.

- Now is the time to explore funding possibilities. Legal training is expensive. You need to make sure that you are fully aware of what you will be getting into.

- Attend law fairs and open days. This is your opportunity to meet representatives of law firms face-to-face and ask questions.

- Attend interviews for periods of recognised training.

- Make sure you apply for a place on the Legal Practice Course.

- Talk to members of the legal profession in order to gain knowledge and guidance and point you in the right direction.

Period of Recognised Training

- The Solicitors Regulation Authority will check that you are suitable at the stage of period of recognised training.

- Sign your contract with the law firm and ensure registration details are sent to SRA.

- If the law firm with which you undertook your period of recognised training with decides not to keep you on, apply for posts as an assistant solicitor.

THE NON-LAW GRADUATE ROUTE

The Non-Law Graduate route, commonly referred to as the conversion route, is another way in which you can train to become a solicitor. Approximately, about 20% of solicitors qualify via this route and follows the key stages as follows:

Degree in any subject – 3 years full time

Common Professional Examination/ Graduate Diploma in Law – 1 year full time, or join the Chartered Institute of Legal Executives (CILEx)

Period of Recognised Training, including the Professional Skills Course – 2 years full time

Admission onto the Roll of Solicitors

Stage 1 – Common Professional Examination/ Graduate Diploma in Law

The Common Professional Examination, or the Graduate Diploma in Law is a course that prepares non-law graduates for the Legal Practice Course. The conversion from one degree to another can be difficult, and will test people's abilities and skills in relation to whether or not they are suitable for changing career paths. This is an intensive course that is built solely on the foundations of law and all the core curriculums and requirements needed to train as a solicitor.

Details of the Legal Practice Course and Period of Recognised Training can be found on the following few pages.

Stage 2 – Vocational Stage – Legal Practice Course

The vocational stage includes the Legal Practice Course and the training contract. Details of the Legal Practice Course and the training contract can be found further on in this chapter.

Stage 3 – Period of Recognised Training

The next step on this path, is to undertake a period of recognised training. This is usually performed over 2 years and this can either be taken whilst completing the vocational LPC stage, or after.

The period of recognised training will enable you to not only put your skills and knowledge to practice, but also to gain further experience, which will help you later on in your career.

Stage 4 – Professional Skills Course (PSC)

This is usually taken when an applicant is undertaking their period of recognised training. It builds on the knowledge and skills that have been acquired throughout the training process of becoming a solicitor.

The Professional Skills Course consists of electives and three core compulsory areas:

- Financial and Business skills
- Advocacy and Communication skills
- Client Care and Professional standards

The compulsory elements of the course involve 48 hours tuition, including assessments, and 24 hours of elective based tuition.

Stage 5 – Admission onto the Roll

Once you have successfully completed all the stages of the law degree route, you can then apply onto the Roll of Solicitors in England and Wales. This entails you to practise as a qualified solicitor.

The Law Degree qualifying Route – Checklist

University

- Apply for a place on the conversion course.

- Make sure that you have arranged funding for the conversion to your law degree.

- Organise work experience and make sure you understand the different types of firms you can work for, and get an idea of the type of lawyer you want to become.

- Prepare your CV carefully.

- Attend law fairs and open days. Be sure to look and act professional. You can meet a lot of important people here, and you want to make a good first impression.

- Apply for a training position in your final year.

GDL / CPE year

- Apply for a place on the Legal Practice Course for the following year.

- Apply for a training position, if not already secured.

- Arrange funding for your LPC course.

THE
CILEx ROUTE

If you have no prior degree but still wish to become a solicitor, you can join CILEx. In order to follow this route, you must first pass examinations to qualify as a member and then later as a fellow. This route takes a long time, is academically challenging and very demanding, and requires that you enter and maintain CILEx-approved legal employment. CILEx's framework for examination allows you to fulfil the requirements of the academic stage of training, including the foundations of legal knowledge.

The CPE/GDL courses cover the foundations of legal knowledge that are required for the completion of the academic stage of training. You may be able to qualify as a solicitor by this route if you don't have a degree, but you need to be a mature student or hold a suitable vocational or academic qualification.

There are two ways in which you can qualify to become a solicitor through the Chartered Institute of Legal Executives (CILEx) – the fellowship route and the membership route.

The membership route – you will be required to undertake a period of recognised training after completing your vocational stages of training.

The fellowship route – this route requires working under supervision for two years after gaining membership. They are therefore exempt from the formal period of recognised training.

In order to qualify for the CILEx route, it is recommended that you have a minimum of 4 GCSEs, including English. If you are not yet working in the legal sector, you can enrol as a student member of the institute, and then take the CILEx Level 3 Professional Diploma in Law before applying for employment.

The CILEx route will take a minimum of 5 years to complete, and you will be required to take the Level 6 Professional Diploma in Higher Law and Practice exam. A CILEx member of the institute will then need to go on and apply for the academic and vocational stages as mentioned above.

THE QUALIFIED LAWYERS TRANSFER SCHEME

Lawyers that qualified in jurisdictions outside of the UK are able to practise in England and Wales as solicitors through the Qualified Lawyers Transfer Scheme (QLTS). The Solicitors Regulation Authority governs the QLTS.

How to Qualify

In order to qualify, a lawyer from another jurisdiction will need to apply for a QLTS certificate of eligibility through the SRA. The certificate is valid for five years and the following requirements will need to be met in order to receive a certificate:

The applicant must have qualified in a SRA recognised jurisdiction. The SRA recognises jurisdictions on the basis that:

• Legal professionals in that jurisdiction are bound by an ethical code that prohibits conflicts of interest and protects the client's interests.

• The jurisdiction's legal education, training and qualifications are at least equivalent to English or Welsh bachelor's degree.

• Lawyers who break that jurisdiction's ethical code can be sanctioned and barred from practice.

The applicant is fully qualified. In order for the SRA to deem a lawyer from a recognised jurisdiction fully qualified, said lawyer will need to be an officer of the court in that jurisdiction and have a right of audience there. The lawyer must also have completed that jurisdiction's general legal education and training programme/programmes, and not be qualified through a specialist or fast-track route.

The applicant will also have to pass SRA assessments on UK legal practice. This step is different depending on if you are a lawyer qualified in the European Economic Area EEA or a lawyer who qualified in jurisdictions outside the EEA. If you qualified outside the EEA jurisdiction, you are known as an 'international applicant'. If you are a UK lawyer (solicitors and barristers who qualified in Scotland, barristers who qualified in England and Wales, and barristers who qualified in Northern Ireland), you are treated in the same way as EEA applicants.

Assessment Format

There are two parts to the QLTS assessments:

1. **Multiple Choice Test (MCT):** This will test knowledge and understanding of the English legal system and European Union Law, professional conduct and solicitors' accounts, constitutional law and judicial review, money laundering and taxation, contract law, financial regulation, criminal law, property law, tort law human rights, equity and trusts and business law. There are 180 questions that are divided into morning and afternoon periods which are three hours each.

2. **Objective Structured Clinical Examination (OSCE):** This will test five skills: *advocacy, interviewing, online legal research writing and drafting*. It is conducted in the context of three practice areas: property law (conveyance and probate, business law and litigation. This test is usually offered over the course of several consecutive days.

In order for you to take the OSCE you must first have passed the MCT. You are not permitted to bring any extra material to the assessments, as the exams are both closed-book exams.

Applicants are given three chances for each part of the QLTS. If any part of the test is failed three times, the applicant must wait five years before reapplying for a certificate and attempting the test again. Applicants will usually have their test results available to them within 12-14 weeks of the assessment date.

Once an applicant has completed and passed the QLTS, and has fulfilled any other requirements set by the SRA, they will be able to apply for admission to the Roll of Solicitors of England and Wales and obtain their practising certificate.

Whatever route you take...

No matter which route you choose to take to become a solicitor, it is necessary for you to complete the Legal Practice Course (LPC). This course will help you develop the skills you will need to work in a firm of solicitors.

The legal sector is more competitive than ever. The number of people that complete the LPC with the hope of becoming a solicitor is much higher than the number of training contracts available across the UK. It is not uncommon for students to be looking for roles several years after completing the LPC.

Legal Practice Course (LPC)

The LPC is a fundamental element of vocational training and will provide you with a general foundation and preparation in aid of your training. In order to begin the LPC, you must have completed the academic training, or be exempt from it, and apply for student membership of the Solicitors Regulation Authority.

The LPC is broadly classified into three phases of learning, "Core" compulsory modules, "Elective" modules, and practical skills. The longest portion of the course that is usually taught in the first portion is the compulsory modules. They are generally:

- Business Law and Practice
- Property Law and Practice
- Criminal Litigation
- Civil Litigation

The shorter second portion of the course, students will select their "Elective" modules. The institution you are attending will provide you a list of electives.

The entire course usually lasts nine months. There is more emphasis placed on classroom teaching and includes independent study. You will usually be given less holiday than you would on an undergraduate course.

Once you have completed the LPC, you will enter the training contract stage of qualification. This stage involves working as a trainee solicitor in a firm of solicitors or another organisation that is authorised to take on trainees. You will be in this stage of qualifying for two years, but if you have previous relevant and suitable legal experience, it can be reduced by up to six months.

Common Professional Examination Course (CPE)

The Common Professional Examination Course is designed to satisfy the academic stage of professional legal education. After passing this course, you will be allowed to move on to the LPC.

The CPE will take place over a 36 week period and will consist of a 7-module course with 140 credits. All of the 'core subjects' will be extensively covered. Generally taught during September, the English Legal System and Legal Method module will give an introduction to the legal system over a four week period. It gives you a background to legal studies.

CPE is designed to satisfy the academics required to become a solicitor.

During lecture classes you will work alongside undergraduates, but during the tutorial classes and the pre-semester course, you will be in CPE small groups. The pre-semester course covers the English Legal System and Legal Method, and takes place over 24 teaching contact hours. Additionally, there will be library exercises, visits to law firms and chambers, guided court visits and career sessions. Other modules include:

- CPE Public Law
- CPE Obligations
- CPE Criminal Law
- CPE Research Training, Interviewing and Advocacy
- CPE EU Law
- CPE Property Law

Graduate Diploma in Legal Studies (GDL)

The Graduate Diploma in Legal Studies is a one year course that will allow non-law graduates to convert to law studies. Once you pass this course, you will be able to move on to the LPC.

This course generally begins two weeks before the autumn semester starts. In order to enter the Diploma course you will have to attend an induction programme and pass a short course.

The GDL is needed if a person wishes to convert their non-law degree and study to become a solicitor.

During the GDL, you will be taking part in seven foundation subjects:

- Constitutional and Administrative Law
- Criminal Law
- Land Law
- Contract Law
- Tort Law
- Law of Trusts
- EU Law

These subjects will be taught through a combination of seminars and lectures, including two lectures a week and a two hour seminar for each subject. You will also be required to complete a 4,000 to 5,000 word research project that will be completed under the supervision of a member of the Faculty. The research project takes place during the second semester and is completed after the final examinations.

Extra-curricular activities are also offered and it is encouraged that you take part in some of those activities.

Final Stages of Qualifying

The final stage to becoming qualified as a solicitor is to pass the Professional Skills Course (PSC). Law graduates and those who have completed the CPE or GDL will attend the PSC while completing the training contract. If you qualify through the CILEx route, you will take the PSC at the end of the route.

The PSC requires the equivalent of 12 days of full-time attendance, building on the vocational training provided in the LPC. There are three core modules:

- Advocacy and communication skills (three days)
- Client care and professional standards (two days)
- Financial and business skills (three days plus exam)

The PSC is the final stage of qualifying to become a solicitor. You are required to complete this, whilst completing your training contract.

You will also be required to obtain 24 hours of elective courses. No more than half of your elective courses can be completed by distance learning. There are a wide range of subject areas, and the courses may be completed any time during the training contract.

Once you have successfully completed all of the qualification stages, you are able to seek admission onto the Roll of Solicitors. After this, you can apply for your first practicing certificate. Every solicitor is subject to continuing professional development requirements.

CHAPTER 8

IMPROVING YOUR CHANCES

Becoming a solicitor is extremely hard work. You need to do your utmost to ensure that you have the best possible start in regards to your legal career. Thus, you want to make sure that you have done everything in your power to better your chances, and ensure you with opportunities and experience that will put you ahead of every other person who is applying for the same job as you.

There a number of ways in which to better your chances, both as a trainee solicitor and as a qualified solicitor. These include:

- Vacation Schemes
- Pro Bono Work
- Westlaw UK
- Law Societies
- Online Forums
- Law Fairs

If you do everything in your power to ensure that you are prepared and ready for the legal world, your application will shine through, and will help put you one step closer to achieving your dream job.

Vacation Schemes

Vacation schemes, also known as vacation placements, are formal periods of work experience within a law firm. They last between one and three weeks. The law sector doesn't usually refer to them as internships, because vacation schemes have the added bonus of a paid cheque of up to £300 per week. Law firms rely on summer, winter and spring vacation schemes to aid them in the recruitment process for training contracts. These vacation placements are offered by most firms if you are a second-year law student and final-year non-law student. There are some exceptions to this, however. Large commercial law firms have recently begun offering insight days for first-year law students.

Why apply for vacation schemes?

Well, quite simply, they will help you get a job. Recruiters want to offer jobs to individuals who show their motivation for a legal career. The ability to list a vacation scheme or two on your CV will show a recruiter that you are motivated and have some consistency in the planning of your career. It is important to note that firms will often interview vacation scheme students for training contract positions towards the end of their placement with the firm. In those cases, the recruiter looks at the vacation placement as a sort of extended interview, where the individual has the opportunity to impress the law firm over an extended period of time.

> Vacation Schemes are a great way to gain experience and enhance your application before applying to law firms.

If you don't get offered a training contract with the firm you did a vacation scheme through, don't fret. This is valuable experience that you can list on your CV, which will help to impress the recruiter. Even if your vacation placement was not in the practice area you wish to enter, it is still great to include in your CV because it shows the recruiter your commitment level to your legal career.

When to apply for a vacation placement?

Generally speaking, 31st January is the most popular deadline if you wish to apply for a summer scheme. Using the autumn term to get organised is important. Here are things that you should do in the autumn term to help prepare for getting a vacation scheme:

- Attend career service events about the legal profession. This can include workshops on campus by law firm representatives.

- Get involved in university clubs and societies. Recruiters look for demonstrations of responsibility, along with interests and activities, in your application so that they can see your ability to juggle priorities. This also helps them to see that you have a well-rounded personality.

- Draft a CV and have it checked by a career adviser. Make sure to reference any legal experience and skills that are transferable to the legal environment.

- Research which firms offer vacation placements. Familiarise yourself with their requirements and application procedures.

- Attend law fairs on campus to talk with recruiters and trainees about your career aspirations. You can also speak to them about their firms.

Law Firms will be impressed if you have taken the extra time to show your commitment to becoming a solicitor.

What to do during the Christmas break and spring term to prepare for getting a vacation scheme:

- Apply for summer vacation placements as early as possible because. Many firms offer spots on vacation schemes before the deadline has closed. If you miss the deadline (generally 31 January), very few firms accept applications in February and March.

- Sign up for recruiter events on campus because they give you an excellent chance to network with recruiters and get their advice.

- Look at building up your work experience. Recruiters often stress how part-time work in retail or bar work can help you to prove that you have the skills to be a lawyer. Include such work on your CV.

- Look into attending open days as they are another opportunity to show your commitment to law.

What to do in the summer term to prepare for getting a vacation scheme:

- Work hard for your exams because recruiters look closely at your academic achievements. High exam results at A-level, and evidence that you are on course for a good 2.1, is important to recruiters. Without a strong academic record, it will be very difficult to secure a training contract.

- Apply for vacation placements with smaller firms.

What to do in the summer break to prepare for getting a vacation scheme:

- If you were unable to get a placement, try a less formal placement at a local, high-street solicitor's firm, or begin enquiring about Christmas placements at big commercial firms.

Pro Bono Work

Pro bono work is ultimately work that lawyers conduct for free. There are many reasons why pro bono work is a plus for solicitors. First of all, whether in a training contract, or in the early years of your law career, pro bono work is beneficial to a solicitor because it gives them experience and helps them to solidify their legal knowledge.

Pro bono work is essentially a way of helping people who are unable to afford legal fees and work for free. Think of it as work experience. The added benefit of pro bono is that it will help a new solicitor to develop the core skills of client care and case management. There are many people who out there, who need help, but just can't afford it. Pro bono work helps with this issue. While you are building your skills doing this type of work, you are helping others in need and allowing others to see the good side of those in the legal profession.

Remember, pro bono work will not only allow you to help those who cannot afford to pay the fees of a solicitor, but it helps you to gain much needed knowledge and skills that will allow you to be a better, more experienced solicitor.

While doing pro bono work, you may find yourself:

- Dealing with local authorities.
- Advising people of the legal complications and consequences of their position.
- Filling in application forms.
- Accompanying a client to a hearing.

Pro bono work is becoming more and more popular among young lawyers. Many law firms are now seeing the benefit of the experience that their solicitors gain in different legal areas when they perform pro bono work. It also helps with the positive image that law firms are trying to exude. There are some law firms that frown upon their solicitors giving pro bono advice. That, however, should not discourage you from doing it. There are plenty of opportunities for you to find pro bono projects outside of the law firm you work for. Pro bono legal advice centres and law clinics are popping up all over the country. These centres and clinics are run by law firms and they are usually very willing to take volunteers from other law firms. By using the pro bono UK website, you can find a project that will suit you best, as well as different agencies.

Many newly qualified and training contract solicitors tend to be extremely busy, thereby making it difficult to decide how much time should be dedicated to pro bono work. That is where the decision is solely yours. Since it is volunteer work, you decide how much time you are willing to donate to the cause. You should only put in as much time as you feel comfortable giving. Any time that you dedicate to helping someone will be much appreciated.

Westlaw UK

Westlaw UK is a system of databases that was created in 2000. These databases contain commentary, news, journal case law, awareness alerts, legislation and EU legal materials. It includes legislation from 1267 to present day as well as nearly 400,000 case reports and transcripts that date back to 1220. In the databases, you will find case law from some of the UK's well known reported series.

Westlaw offers practice area specific, services and current awareness that is updated every 15 minutes. They offer analytical commentary from the entire Common Law Library, and also offer a range of market-leading books.

> Westlaw UK is a database that contains news and case laws to improve your knowledge and skills.

Once a member, you will be able to save your research in very manageable folders on their site, and set up alerts. It has been optimized for your smart phone and tablet. They even offer intranet solutions for customised knowledge management systems.

As a solicitor, this service will ensure that, as you research for cases that you are working on, you will have access to the most relevant data available. Not only do you have access to these very useful databases through Westlaw UK, but you are also offered the opportunity to take their certification training which gives you an interactive walk-through of their system. Once you have done the training, you will then be given the option to test what you have learned and become certified.

If you choose to get certified and pass the test, you will be sent your certificate in the post, and will be able to use this on your CV. Having access to all of this information as well as being certified will show future employers just how serious you are about being a solicitor.

Westlaw UK Basic Certification

This training and certification will provide you with an introduction to Westlaw UK. It will cover effective searching, refining results and using status icons to ensure that you are using good law. It is recommended that you complete all of the Basic modules before you attempt to take the Basic test. There are four parts to the Basic Certification:

- Part 1: Getting Started
- Part 2: Primary Law
- Part 3: Secondary Sources
- Part 4: Basic Certification Test

Westlaw UK Advanced Certification

In order to move on to the Advanced Certification, you will have to take and pass Basic Certification. This certification covers Boolean search connectors, legislative modification and derivation tables, judicial consideration of case law, as well as EU and other advanced topics.

Westlaw International Training Module

This training will cover the skills you will need to find global legal information on Westlaw International.

Going through the training and getting certified is beneficial to all solicitors. Since you have access to case law dating back to the 1200s, you have the opportunity to research and possibly set a new precedence. You will have the knowledge at your fingertips to represent your clients to the fullest. With updates made every 15 minutes, you will have access to the most recent information to help you move yourself further in your career. Having the skill and the access that Westlaw UK offers will be a welcome addition to your CV.

Law Societies

Law societies are professional organisations that represent solicitors. Many offer Continuing Professional Development (CPD) training to their members. Aside from this training, becoming a member of a law society gives you another great opportunity to network with other members. Societies will often offer opportunities to meet with other members at several different functions.

Local law societies offer their members the benefit of networking with other solicitors in their area, in turn giving them the opportunity to perhaps send a client to another solicitor who specialises in their needed area.

Law Societies are organisations that represent solicitors. It provides another great way of getting connected with a range of different people.

Through The Law Society, there are eight regional branches:

- Law Society in the Eastern Region
- Law Society in Greater London
- Law Society in the Midlands
- Law Society of the North East
- Law Society of the North West
- Law Society of the South East
- Law Society of the North East
- Law Society of Yorkshire

Online Forums

Online forums give not only the public, but also solicitors a place to get current, relevant information on many topics. If you show law firms that you have been researching wider issues, and are engaging with the legal issues within society; it demonstrates your determination and willingness to go that extra mile. Remember, the legal sector is a competitive industry, and thus you need to make sure you are doing everything you can to ensure you have the edge over other candidates.

Online Forums allow you to view the profiles of solicitors throughout the UK, hold discussions about important subjects and put yourself out there for others to find.

It is a great networking tool. Law forums also give the public a place to go and get free legal advice. This is a great way to gain potential clients, off the back of your own, helpful tips.

> Online Forums are a great way to get connected and gain information on a range of legal topics.

There are a vast number of online forums that focus on law. You can find forums based on the area of practice you are concentrating on as well as general forums. Below you will find a list of just some of the forums that are out there to help you along the way:

- TraineeSolicitor.co.uk (to find a training contract or just talk about training contracts)
- TheLawForum.co.uk
- FindLaw UK
- Professional Forum for UK Solicitors (LinkedIn)

Law Fairs

Law fairs are a great way to better your chances and get yourself noticed. These are specialist career fairs which enable people the opportunity to find out more about law careers, and help you decide where you would best fit in.

You can find a list law fairs at the following web address: lawcareers.net.

Who should attend?

These fairs are highly recommended for law students in their second year of study. They will help you gain vacation scheme placements, work experience, and even training contracts.

> Law Fairs are your chance to meet people from law firms, ask questions, get yourself noticed and gain as much information as you can regarding your potential career.

Why attend a law fair?

Law fairs allow you to find out about different types of legal work and gain valuable insight and information from qualified legal professionals. It's a great step to get a feel and an insight about what law firms are about, what they expect and what's on offer. Some recruiters use law fairs as part of their recruitment process, and whilst you are unlikely to walk away with a training contract, it might happen.

Here are some useful tips on attending a law fair:

1. **Plan which law firms you would like to meet.** By going to your law department or career service department on campus, you should be able to obtain a list of law firms that will have exhibits at the campus fair. Researching the firms and getting an idea of

which ones seem to appeal to you more than others is a great way to prepare for the day.

2. **Show off your research.** Having researched law firms ahead of time, you will have a head start to impressing the recruiters. You will know where they are located, what areas of law they specialise in and some top cases they have worked on, as well as how they are progressing as a company. Knowing important facts about the law firm will show the recruiters that you took the time to research them. If you impress the recruiter, you are more likely to be asked to contact them regarding a vacation scheme or training contract.

3. **Never ask a recruiter why you should apply to their firm.** This will make you sound arrogant. They are not there to be interviewed; you are there to hopefully be asked to an interview. You should, however, ask questions regarding their culture, training and application process. If you would really like to impress the recruiter you could ask them about opportunities for early responsibility.

4. **Show up looking the part of a solicitor.** Even at a law fair on campus, first impressions count. If you are dressed in jeans and a t-shirt, the recruiters will have a hard time picturing you in your new role as a solicitor. Dress the part. Wear what you would be expected to wear while representing an important client.

5. **Confidence is key.** It is important that prospective employers see you as a confident individual. No matter how nervous you may be, you should still hold yourself in a manner that shows them that you are proud to be in the field. Keep your head up, your shoulders back, offer a firm hand to shake, and speak in an even tone.

6. **Speak with current trainee solicitors.** At most law fairs, you will find trainee solicitors. This may be one of your only chances to ask questions about being a trainee. By asking questions, you will be able to get a first-hand account of what the realities are of life at a firm.

7. **Follow up with recruiters after the fair.** If you were able to form a good rapport with any recruiters at the fair, contacting them afterwards will show them initiative. Send them an email thanking them for the opportunity to talk to them. Thank them for taking the time out of their schedule and going out of their way to be helpful. Recruiters talk to a lot of people at fairs and it is hard for them to remember everyone they speak to. By sending them an email after the fair, they will have a record of who you are.

CHAPTER 9

TRAINING CONTRACTS AND OPPORTUNITIES

A training contract is based on a period of recognised training; the final stage of the qualifying process. Once you have completed the LPC, you will enter the training contract stage of qualification. This stage involves working as a trainee solicitor in a firm of solicitors or another organisation that is authorised to take on trainees. You will be in this stage of qualifying for two years, but if you have previous relevant and suitable legal experience, it can be reduced by up to six months.

Think of your training contract as an apprenticeship. It will provide you with two years of opportunities and valuable experience that allow you to expand your horizons and improve your performance. What you will learn, and what you will be doing within your training contract, will ultimately depend on the type of law firm for which you have applied. If you join a large firm, you are likely to spend your time in a range of different seats (departments) giving you an all-round feel to the possibilities open to you after your training contract has ended.

Training Contracts are your way to put everything you have learned up until now into good practice in a law firm.

During the training contract, you will be required to undertake the Professional Skills Course. After successfully completing a training contract, a trainee solicitor can then seek admission onto the Roll of Solicitors and apply for their practising certificate.

What to expect?

The training contract, including the Professional Skills Course (PSC), is the stage that allows you to put all your preparation, knowledge and skills into practice and develop as a solicitor within a law firm.

Normally, in larger firms, you can expect to spend four blocks of six months in different departments (these are usually called 'seats').

So, in other words, within your two years training, you generally spend six months in one seat, before rotating to another seat, i.e. another department.

In smaller firms, this can vary. The amount of rotations you take in one seat will depend on the law firm which you have applied to. The Solicitors Regulation Authority however, does require trainee solicitors to cover at least three different areas.

In 2014, the SRA made some adaptions to the training contracts and education policies. The SRA no longer stipulates the exact terms and conditions of a person's training contract, and therefore law firms have been given the freedom to design their own training programme which they see beneficial for their firm.

Remember, many law firms tend to want to keep trainee solicitors on after their training contract. So, make sure you perform at your best to ensure the best possible opportunities and potential long-term career with that law firm.

Where to look for a training contract?

The majority of large firms recruit online, you should do your utmost to research into the law firm for which you are applying. You can keep ahead of the competition if you take the time and effort to understand what makes a good application and how to improve your chances of gaining a Training Contract.

- Make good use of recruitment events such as law fairs and read up on what recruiters have to offer you, as well as illustrating what you have on offer.

- Match your skills to the qualities and attributes required from different law firms. Remember, every law firm will be looking for something different.

Top Five Tips to Improve Your Chances of Getting a Training Contract

1. **Work Experience.** Without work experience, you will not progress in your legal career.

2. **Perfect your CV and Application For Answers.** Spelling mistakes, lack of information, poor layout, grammatical errors, incorrect information and offering nothing substantial to an employer, are the most common mistakes on a CV and job application. Make sure you have someone else go over your CV.

3. **Make Sure You Have A Great Cover Letter.** Your cover letter is your chance to let the employer know about you and why you want to work for them. Do your research about the firm so you can be sure that your cover letter tells them you have what it takes to be a solicitor for their firm.

4. **Give Yourself An Interesting Persona.** Simply stating on your CV that you like to read or watch movies will make you seem boring to an interviewer. There is nothing wrong with going sky-diving and listing that as a hobby. There are so many hobbies out there that show personality, and if you do it once, you can list it as something that interests you. Make yourself interesting and exciting.

5. **Consider Your Location.** Because the competition is so tight in this field, people are willing to travel far and wide to get a position. There is no rule that says you have to state your address on your CV. If you have relatives near a firm you are interested, feel free to use their address. This gives you a tie to the area.

CHAPTER 10

THE IMPORTANCE OF BEING CONNECTED

What is networking?

Networking is a great way to get your name out there. It is an extremely useful way to build up your contacts and build on your opportunities in terms of your legal career.

Once you have completed the qualification process and have begun working as a solicitor, your next task will be ongoing. You will begin the important process of 'Networking'. Networking is a fundamental skill that will help you to ensure that your career goals are achieved. Whether you are a trainee or a senior partner, an important part of your job will be in business development. You are now responsible for helping the organisation/firm to grow. Networking helps to spread the word about you and your firm. Networking will also help you to gain new information and knowledge about changing laws or practices.

Networking is a way of reaching out to people. There are three steps to this process:

- Meeting somebody for the first time.
- Building a rapport with somebody new and getting them to like you.
- Creating trust on an initial basis.

If you can meet someone new and not only get to know them but get them to trust you, you have one more person to help add to your knowledge bank.

Why should you be networking?

It is important to understand that networking is a crucial step to becoming a successful solicitor. Trainee solicitors gain valuable experience through networking experienced and professional lawyers, and putting themselves on the legal map in the process.

If you want to be considered a professional lawyer who takes their job seriously, then networking is a must.

Networking is a very important task that will be expected of you as you grow in your career as a solicitor and as you grow in the firm for which you work. Not only will it help your firm with business development, it will help you progress.

By networking, you will be able to:

- Build your confidence.
- Discover professional lawyers who can offer you help, give you advice and point you in the right direction, in terms of your legal career.
- Build up social relations and connect with people who are in a similar position to your own.

- Expand your legal horizons, via outside knowledge, experience, communication, professionalism and connections.

It is true by the saying that: it's not what you know but who you know. Although this seems like a really unfair strategy, the truth behind it is inevitable. Nobody can argue that no matter how good you are and how experienced you may be, certain jobs are hard to come by. Knowing where to look is the first step in understanding how to get the job you want. However, it is even more important to appreciate that having your name out there, puts you one step closer to achieving your goal.

You will be surprised by the amount of word of mouth recommendations, which circulates within the legal sector. Getting connected with other people in the same position you are, or solicitors of more qualified status, ensures you are fully prepared for the world of legal aid, and gaining support and advise through other legal professionals is invaluable to your success.

Stay connected. If you take the time and make new contacts, be sure to stay in contact with them. Follow up on anyone who accepts you as a friend or has followed you.

How to network?

There are many avenues available for you to explore. Social media is quickly becoming a growing method for business networking across the world. One of the most important social networking tools for law professionals, is LinkedIn.

LinkedIn

Having a profile on LinkedIn will allow you to brand yourself, showcase your skills and accomplishments, and build and manage your network. Once you have a LinkedIn account, you will be able to find others in your field and browse their profiles. This will help you to see how you rank amongst others.

While using LinkedIn, or any other social media avenue, it is important to consider your level of professionalism. You never want to come across as a solicitor whose priorities lie outside of the law world. Be careful of posting content that could make you look unprofessional, or potentially unreliable as an employee.

This is the time to make an impression. LinkedIn is a great way to build up your networking system, and use it to help you contact other professionals. LinkedIn is used at a business and professional level that, if you put the time and effort on your profile, you will prosper in terms of your career.

Other avenues include networking events specifically designed to encourage groups of solicitors to get connected, and interact with each other. When searching for a training contract, you may go to a job fair. This is in essence, networking. You are putting yourself out there, talking to people, getting them to trust you and eventually, getting them to offer you a training contract. That is career development. The same applies for business development. While working for a firm, you are expected to get yourself noticed, mingle at functions, talk to other solicitors and get your firms name out there and

Katie Noakes
Student at Canterbury Christ Church University

Rochester, United Kingdom | Marketing and Advertising

Education   Canterbury Christ Church University

✎ Add Experience ❓

View profile as ▾

on the map. How do you expect people to come to you with their legal issues if they have never heard of you? This is the time in your life when you must be most professional. You definitely would not want a prospective employer or client to see a side of you that was in the past but that could potentially ruin your chances.

It takes some practice for those who are not accustomed to this, but if you plan to work with people you do not know on a daily basis, networking at functions will help you gain the confidence to communicate with your clients comfortably and confidently.

On a personal level, networking will also benefit you. You are now putting in a lot of hours and dedicating your life to a new career in the legal world. Networking with other solicitors may introduce you to those that you will form friendships with. They will understand your crazy schedule and likely help you to cope with the stresses of your new career.

Never try to portray yourself as being something other than what you are. Be yourself, but let your future employer know that you can be moulded into the perfect fit for their firm.

USEFUL TIPS FOR NETWORKING

- Stay connected with everyone you get into contact with. Make sure that you take the time to keep active on your networking accounts.

- Make yourself noticed. The more you put yourself out there, the more likely you are to get noticed by someone.

- Keep active. Make sure that you are frequently checking your networking sites. Not only will this work to your advantage, but it will keep you up-to-date with any changes or new contacts that you might receive.

- Use more than one networking method. Consider all the types of social networking sites: Facebook, Twitter, LinkedIn; the more ways you are connected, the more chance you have of being found.

- Connect with everyone. Do not dismiss someone because you think they are irrelevant. If you dismiss someone, you might lose out on an opportunity. The more diverse you are with your contacts, the more ways in which you will be able to find what you are looking for.

- Sending emails is a great way to get you started. Take the time to carefully construct a clear and appealing email that someone will want to take the time to read.

- Remember, be professional. You only get one chance to make a first impression, and you don't want that impression to let you down and stop you making that all important con-tact. Be professional, mature, experienced – portray yourself as serious and motivated.

CHAPTER 11

BUILDING YOUR CV

Finding the right law firm to work at will just be one of the hurdles you will face upon the completion of your education. You will want to apply for jobs at multiple firms, but in order to be considered for any job, you must have a proper CV.

What is a CV?

Before creating your CV and cover letter, you should first research the company you are applying for a job with. This will help you to know which of your skills you will want to highlight according to what they are looking for.

CV stands for 'Curriculum Vitae', and is otherwise known as a Resume. Your CV tells a future employer everything they need to know about you, in order to make an informed decision as to whether or not you are the right person for the position. It is the most important marketing tool you will use to help sell yourself, so you need to understand the importance of conducting a great CV.

- Make sure that it is easy to read, clearly laid out in a logical order, and that you haven't tried to cram in too much. Usually 2 pages is sufficient enough.

- Make sure that it is informative and that it isn't cluttered with irrelevant information.

- Make sure that you account for any gaps in your employment history. For example, if you were traveling or took time off to further your education, you should list those instances.

- Make sure that you include your entire schooling history including dates and grades. If you leave your grades off, the employer will be left to assume that they are sub-par.

- Make sure that you include your qualification date, either confirmed or pending, and the jurisdiction. (Also include whether you require or hold a visa to work in the UK).

- Make sure that you include any extra training courses you have taken and any articles you have written or contributed to, as well as any seminars or marketing activities you have been involved in.

- If you belong to any societies, make sure you include those memberships as well.

- If you have taken and passed the certification process for Westlaw, include this certification.

- Make sure that it is free of grammatical and spelling errors.

Along with specific things you should do to make your CV effective, there are also a number of things you should NOT do:

- Don't use the words CV or Resume on your document. The employer knows what it is, and it takes up valuable space that could be used to show your talent.

- Don't make your CV more than two pages long. Generally speaking, a potential employer will be busy and will not have time to read a lengthy history.

- Don't include work experience that is not relevant to the position you are applying for.

- Don't exaggerate your educational or work experience. If you do so, you will likely be found out at some point.

- Don't include personal information such as religion, marital status, ethnicity or age.

- Don't have your CV printed on both sides of a page. Each page is important and should be on its own sheet of paper.

- Don't fold your CV. A clean, creaseless CV is more appealing to the eye. Keep your CV in a folder so that you can hand it to a potential employer. If you are mailing a CV, mail it in an envelope large enough that you will not need to fold it.

Formatting Your CV

It is important to format your CV in a way that is pleasing to the reader's eyes. Before they even know who the CV belongs to, they will scan over the document and form opinions about you just on the way you have presented yourself on paper.

It is well known by advertising and marketing agencies that people scan the page first. They do this diagonally, not linearly. They will first look at the top left of the page, but their gaze will move down the page to the bottom right corner.

Generally you will have between three and six seconds to grab their attention enough to keep them reading. If you give them a list of points, but have not grabbed their attention by the end of the third point, it is almost guaranteed that they will move on to another part of the page. There are a few things you can do to grab the attention of a future employer:

- You can change the font, but it is not a good idea to use more than two types of font.
- You can change the font size.
- You can change the font colour, but it is not recommended to use more than two colours.

CV Examples

The following pages contain examples of CV's, specifically tailored to future solicitors. While the first example does not list personal interests, the second sample does. Your interests make you a bit more human, and adding them to your CV will make you seem more personable. If you list your interests, keep the list short and to the point. Do not make your list too long or the employer may feel you will not have adequate time to dedicate to the position you are applying for.

(Sample A)

Name	Andrew McDonnell
Contact Details	(address)
	(telephone number)
	(email address)
Nationality	British
Visa Status	Not required
Admitted	To be admitted as a Solicitor in England & Wales, March 2011
Languages	Italian (fluent), French (fluent), German (basic)

Education	2007-2008	College of Law, London LPC – Commendation
	2004-2007	University of Nottingham LLB (Hons) – 2:1
	2002-2004	Loughborough High School 4 A-Levels (AABB) 10 GCSEs (6A*s, 2As, 2Bs)

Employment History

March 09 to Present   City Law Firm LLP, London
Trainee Solicitor

Training seats undertaken in:

- Banking & Capital Markets (Sep 2010 - present) including 3 months secondment to Investment Bank.
- Corporate (Mar 2010 – Sep 2010)
- Commercial Property (Sep 2009 – Mar 2010)
- Construction Litigation (Mar 2009 – Sep 2009)

Banking Capital Markets

- Secondment to Investment Bank – assisting with a variety of matters that included novations, securitization/asset swaps and totally return swaps, as well as CDS deliverability analyses.

- Various bond issuances for leading investment banks including a number of repurchases and amendments for a leading European Investment Bank.

- Assisted with the drafting of several bilateral and syndicated loan agreements.

- Liaised with the bank and solicitors on the other side in both asset-based lending and acquisition finance transitions.

Corporate

- Acted for an international energy company on its AIM IPO

- Conducted due diligence for share and business acquisitions

- Drafted a response to a request for preliminary information and compiled a due diligence bundle for the share purchase of a lift installation and maintenance company. Also amended said share purchase agreement.

- Acted for an international DIY company, involving the drafting of confidentiality agreements, licence agreements and employment contracts.

- Acted for a private equity house on the sale of a national recruitment company in which it was the majority shareholder. Led the due diligence and disclosure letter exercises, assisted with the drafting of the sale and purchase agreement and played an active role in the completion negotiations.

- Acted for a UK entrepreneur on the acquisition and financing of a water purification company (large-scale private equity investment).

Commercial Property

- Acted for the landlord in the renewal of a court-protected lease to a nationwide household goods franchise. Attended client meetings, drafted a side letter with regard to insurance provisions and liaised with the clients surveyors. Drafted a new lease incorporating the terms from the original lease, a Deed of Variation and heads of Terms.

- Acted for the vendor in the sale of the freehold of unregistered shop premises to the incumbent tenant in rent arrears. Investigated and calculated rent arrears, drafted the contract for sale.

Construction Litigation

- Part of a team advising on a large-scale construction arbitration. Worked extensively with one of the main witnesses in the proceedings. Extensive time spent on witness preparation for cross-examination and drafting the Witness Statement.

- Worked on an adjudication involving a developer and contractor. Drafted the Statement of Case within an accelerated adjudication time frame and was heavily involved in evidence gathering.

- Assisted with a major arbitration between contractors, architects, developers and a Local Authority. Conducted research, attended fact finding meetings and drafted Statement of Defence and Counterclaim.

	August 2008 West End Law LLP
	To Jan 2009 Paralegal
	Worked as a paralegal in the property department, assisting the senior partner with commercial and residential property transactions.
Additional Information	Contributor to articles Attended external course on marketing

(Sample B)

Nicolas Johnson
(Address)
(Telephone)
(E-mail address)

Overview

- Admitted as a solicitor in December 2003 having been called to the Bar by Lincoln's Inn in November 2001
- Advises in all areas of property litigation, including landlord and tenant matters, possession, trespass, insolvency as it relates to property and development disputes

Education

- Oxford Grammar School
- LLB Law (Hons), University of Manchester
- BVC, Inns of Court School of Law
- PGDL, City University
- QLTT, BPP Law School

Qualified

22.11.01 Barrister (Lincoln's Inn)
17.12.03 Solicitor

Career

Mid-Tier Law Firm LLP – 2003 to present

- Advising clients on alienation of leases, including the transfer of leases held by OK supermarkets to independent retailers and the sale of several London restaurants, including X, Y, Z and T.

- Acting for the landlords in ABCLimited v Good Stores Limited in successfully obtaining an injunction to require the tenant and a third party to surrender an under lease that was entered into without consent.

- Representing StarsJupiter in resisting a claim for an injunction based on alleged rights of light to restrain the construction of a strategically important residential development in the City of London. Confidential settlement terms which enabled completion of the development were agreed immediately before trial.

- Acting for the claimant in GenProp Limited v XYZLimited in successfully defeating the defendant's application for summary judgment against GenProp's claim for an injunction to restrain the defendants from using dry dock facilities on the River Thames in breach of a deed of covenant and substantial damages. The claim was later settled during trial on terms that the defendants would be subject to an injunction, and would pay damages and costs.

- Advising a developer in relation to a claim for increased overage payments by a borough council following the regeneration and redevelopment of Trowbridge, Hackney.

- Representing clients, including OK Hotels and StarsJupiter (see above) against property professional, including solicitors.

- Advising clients including ABC Estate and XYZ Offices Group in relation to portfolio management, including in particular landlord and tenant/development issues.

- Representing private client in relation to a substantial claim against insurers for non-payment under an insurance policy following subsidence damage, and in a claim against a damp proofing company.

Barrister (non-practising) – 2001 to 2003

- Landlord and tenant possession claims
- Consumer credit repossessions
- Mortgage possession claims
- Enforcement proceedings
- Small claims hearings
- Applications for summary judgment and to set aside judgment
- Bankruptcy proceedings

Mid-Tier Firm Paralegal – 2001

- General employment/civil litigation advice

Interests
- Sport
- Travel
- History

As you can see, both samples are quite different from one another, but they both include clear, concise, grammatically correct information. Both are two pages long, and neither lists any information that would be considered inappropriate or unnecessary.

Remember to keep it simple when creating your CV.

Again, your CV is a marketing tool. You are trying to sell yourself to a prospective employer. If you are planning on applying for different types of jobs, you may want to create a couple of CVs. You want your CV to be pertinent to the job for which you are applying. Don't be afraid to list many accomplishments. It will not be showing off, as long as the accomplishments pertain to the job you are seeking.

Remember to keep it simple when creating your CV. Too many colours or fonts may make the CV look unprofessional, and the type of font you choose should be clean and easy to read. Leave out information that does not directly pertain to the position, and only use wording that sounds professional.

When applying for a job, always keep in mind the specification listed for the role. You should make a list of the requirements, and then check over your CV to make sure you have shown that you meet these necessities. Not all firms will expect the exact same set of skills or expertise, so researching each firm individually to learn exactly what they will expect from a new hire is extremely important. This being said, be prepared to re-design your CV to suit each position you apply for.

Use the information you obtained during your research as a blueprint for writing your CV. You are more likely to be called in for an interview if you match what an employer is looking for. If you provide an employer with a professional, clearly written and thought out CV, they will feel confident that you possess the skills, behaviour, experience and morals that they are looking for.

As stated above, you want your CV to be a reflection of the skills you possess, and how they will help you to perform the job you are applying for.

CHAPTER 12

THE SOLICITOR APPLICATION FORM

By the time you reach the stage of applying for a period of recognised training, you should by now, know what type of law firm you wish to work for, and the type of lawyer you want to be. Within this chapter, you will be provided with guidance and support in preparation of your all-important application form.

The application form is one of the most crucial stages to the application process of becoming a solicitor. The level of research and the effort which needs to be put into your application form is imperative. When submitting application forms, it is important to produce a quality, professional and detailed application form which will make you stand out. It is the first time that you will get to make an impression and set yourself apart from other candidates.

In terms of application forms, a lot of law firms rely solely on the application format in which they have laid out, as opposed to allowing candidate's to attach their CV. The main aim of the application form is for law firms to be given all the necessary information which they want. Take note that application forms are often long winded and can be quite daunting. The forms ask for a great deal of detail and research, so it is absolutely essential that your response is highly driven, full of detailed information, and clearly illustrates all your best abilities.

Common application questions

The key thing to remember when filling out application forms is that every law firm is different, and therefore they will expect different responses. Whilst the majority of application questions remain similar and assess certain attributes, it is important to tailor each application specifically to the law firm for which you are applying to.

The application form is one of the most crucial stages to the application process of becoming a solicitor.

We have listed some of the most common application form questions, and provided you with a sample answer below each question, so that you can get a good idea of how to respond:

- Why have you chosen law?

"A job in law is a noble profession that allows a person to not only build on their skills and knowledge, but it also provides satisfaction and enjoyment in providing a service that solves legal matters for a range of people. I feel as though I have the capacity to provide a fantastic service to people who need my help".

- Which other law firms have you applied for, and why?

If you have applied for other law firms, don't lie! Chances are the law firm is testing you and are likely in contact with other law firms. They will find you out. Make sure that if you have applied to other law firms, you elaborate on why you value this law firm over others. You want to demonstrate your priority towards that particular law firm. Showing a keen interest for a firm makes recruiters more likely to employ you.

- Why have you chosen to apply to our law firm?

"After extensive research, I believe that your law firm is a highly successful business that builds trusting relationships with their clients through a service that is committed, professional and prosperous. I believe that my skills are tailored to your firm and I am certain that I can bring a lot to your company, as well as learning invaluable skills and knowledge from established professionals such as yourself."

- Tell us about your most significant achievements.

"The fact that I have come this far in terms of my legal career is an exciting prospect. I have relished every learning curve the law has so far offered me, and I hope to expand my horizons within the legal industry and put my skills, knowledge and experience to the test. A significant achievement is ultimately completing my law

degree and having the determination and will power to continue my journey in law."

- Give examples of work experience relevant to a career in the law industry.

"Whilst completing my legal studies, I did my utmost to ensure I gained relevant work experience that will help on my journey to becoming a lawyer. I took it upon myself to gain several weeks work experience at a law firm which allowed me to gain a feel for what I could expect if I decided to pursue this career. I also participated in the Vacation Scheme whereby it provided formal experience and understanding regarding the world of the legal profession".

Covering letter

When applying to a job by mail or even through a firm's website, you will need to include a cover letter. Your cover letter gives a first impression to any employer, and will explain your reasons for becoming a solicitor and why you are applying to their firm. In order for your cover letter to be effective, you must have a clear structure. It is not uncommon for employers to read a cover letter and not even go on to look at the CV or job application. You must impress them first with your cover letter and make them want to know more about you.

If you are applying for a training contract, your cover letter will want to include the following:

- **The opening.** This is an introduction and here you should explain what stage you are at in your studies, including what university you are attending. Here you would state that you are applying for a training contract. You will also explain where you saw their advertisement. This portion of your cover letter should only be one or two sentences.

- **Why?** Your second paragraph should explain why you want to be a solicitor and why you wish to work for that law firm. Here you would also explain any experiences you've had that brought you to the decision to be a solicitor. This may include vacation schemes and even mini-pupillages. Doing so will impress recruiters when they see the effort you put forth into comparing the two sides of the legal profession. You should also make it clear why you want to work in the area of law that the firm focuses on. This is a great chance to show off any research you did about the firm, by explaining your interest in their main practice areas. Also, draw on your experience you may have working at other commercial firms. Be sure to provide evidence of your interest.

- **Why you?** This is the section where you get to pitch yourself to the recruiter. You will want to make it clear that you are suited to a career as a solicitor. Highlight any achievements that show you have the competence they are looking for. If your cover letter is attached to an actual job application, be careful to only repeat information you filled out on the application that is most significant. Be as broad as possible.

- **The ending.** Here you want to close your letter, referring the recruiter to your CV and stating your availability for an interview.

Overall, your cover letter should be no longer than one page. Keep it professional, using a font size of 11 or 12. Never rush to send it to the recruiter. Make sure you go over the letter several times, ensuring that there are no spelling or grammatical errors. Ask friends or family to read over the letter, and suggest any improvements. This will ensure that the cover letter is professional, clean and accurate.

The point of a covering letter is to highlight the reasoning why you are applying for the job position. Information that you should focus on within a covering letter is:

- Why you have chosen to become a solicitor?
- Why you have applied for this firm?
- Why you make a good candidate? Skills, experience, qualities.
- Other interests and skills that enhance your application.

(Sample Cover Letter for Application into Training Contract)

Name
Street Address
City of Residence

Date

Name of recruiter/employer (if available)
Name of firm
Street Address
City firm is located

Dear Mr./Ms. _____/Dear Sir/Madam,

I am writing to apply for a Training Contract at (Name of law firm) as advertised on your graduate recruitment website. Currently, I am in the second year of my law degree at Birmingham University.

While at university, I have sought out experiences that are relevant to a career as a solicitor. Recently, I undertook a three-day insight placement at XXX Law Firm. There I shadowed a trainee in a property law seat and also spoke with partners from other areas of practice in order to broaden my knowledge of working as a solicitor. In addition, I also had a two-week placement at the high street firm XYZ, where I was able to observe solicitors as they acted for local businesses that wished to expand. While in this placement, I was commended for the commercial aware ness I displayed in highlighting the potential disadvantages of-said acquisition when asked to draw up a list of relevant issues affecting a chain of vet surgeries purchasing another practice.

After comparing these experiences to my time spent in open court sessions at Norfolk County Court, I believe that I am well suited to a career at a City law firm and wish to further expand my experience in this environment.

Multi-jurisdictional mergers and acquisitions are where my interests lie, and I have been following the expansion of UK law firms into new territories like Australia and Morocco. While speaking with solicitors from your firm in this field at graduate recruitment events, I found that I am very interested in finding out more about your firm's M&A seat, and would love the opportunity to speak with your current trainees about their experiences working with overseas offices. I further believe that my skills in the French and Spanish languages will benefit me when dealing with colleagues in your French and Spanish offices.

Working as a customer services assisting at LMNO's has enhanced my ability to work well with clients. Whilst there, my ability to build a rapport with customers earned me a quick promotion. I have put this skill to work in my role as a student manager of the university legal advice clinic, where I persuade local law firms to supply solicitors. I am also president of the university law society and have arranged guest speakers, including Peter Lodder QC. By collaborating with other members of the Law Society committee, we have increased the society's membership by 30 percent within six months.

Please find my CV attached. I am available for an interview at any time, and I very much look forward to your response.

Yours sincerely,
(Your name)

Remember, you must tailor your answers to each application you fill out in a different way. Each law firm has its own unique style and so, what fits for one firm, maybe slightly different to another.

Law firms use application forms as a constructive tool to filter out the strong candidates from those less desirable. Thus, you need to make sure that your application form is the best it can be. Law firms want to see that you have thoroughly researched their company, you show sheer determination and willingness to preserve and progress, they want to see potential candidates who show the commitment, knowledge and understanding of the expectations required to be a successful lawyer.

Make sure you spend a lot of time on your application form. You want to make sure that you present yourself in the best way possible. This includes choosing the right work experience, highlighting achievements, attributes and qualities gained etc.

If you are already a practising solicitor in search of a new job, you would follow the same route, leaving out the portion of the cover letter that states what university you are attending and what year of schooling you are in. Instead, you would inform the recruiter/employer of how many years of experience you hold.

Tips for Filling out Applications

- Prepare yourself by doing research on the firm/organisation and their recruitment criteria.

- Be clear on the selection criteria and try to match your skills, experience and knowledge.

- Read through the entire form and follow the instructions exactly as stated.

- Gauge your answers to fit the space provided.

- Do a rough draft to make sure that you can fit your information into the boxes.

- Online forms will specify a word count; this indicates how much detail is required.

- Make sure that your application is neat. Trying to cram information in by writing small shouldn't be done.

- Don't leave gaps on the application. If you travelled for a period of time instead of holding a job, put that down.

Common Mistakes to Avoid When Filling Out Application Forms

- Spelling mistakes. In general, most firms have found that it is rare to find a job application without a spelling error. Check and re-check to ensure you spelled everything right.

- Not going into the amount of detail requested on the application. If the academic portion asks for your grades, they want all of your grades, not just the ones you feel most comfortable giving.

- Skipping a question on the application. On a lot of applications, a question will be asked that actually has multiple parts. Commonly, some parts get skipped. If the question is asking for five pieces of information, make sure you answer all five parts of the question.

- Giving too much negative information because there was space to fill out on the form. If you are asked for extenuating circumstances about an academic result and you spend three paragraphs telling about your bout with a stomach virus (in detail) that led you to have a bad grade the company is less likely to employ you. Try to be as positive and informative as possible without being longwinded.

- Using examples from your personal life, instead of your work life. If you are asked to describe a time that you had to be part of a team and overcome a problem, they don't want to hear about how you and your siblings had to plan an anniversary party for your parents and only had two days to do it.

- Feeling the need to fill up every space. If there is a large space to fill, you don't necessarily have to fill up every inch. Give a sufficient answer, but don't feel you have to keep going just because there is still space in the section.

- Waffling. This is done on many applications. It is the act of using business jargon to fill space without actually saying anything important.

- Filling boxes with irrelevant detail when asked for specific answers. If you were asked about positions of responsibility, the employer doesn't need to hear about how you were the person responsible in your class for turning on the lights and handing out the books at the start of class. They want to hear about relevant work responsibilities.

- Using the 'Any Other Information' section to spew nonsense. It will be completely useless to fill this section out with little bits of information that jump all over the place. Use this section to tell them additional information about you that they have not already asked in the application. This should be information that is relevant to the job you are applying for.

CHAPTER 13

THE INTERVIEW PROCESS

Getting an interview has become harder than ever, in recent years. Competition is fierce and therefore you need to be fully prepared and demonstrate that you are at your best. Nobody enjoys the interview process, in fact the majority of people find the whole experience nerve-wracking. You will need to show great levels of knowledge and experience within the law industry, and have a good understanding of the job role you are applying for. If you prepare for the interview, and emphasise your skills and abilities effectively, you have a great chance of getting any job.

Generally speaking, many newly-qualified solicitors would rather stay with the firm where they trained. This is because they are familiar with the staff and the way things are done. They would have built up a rapport with the company and gained an understanding as to what is expected. It is also common that the firm would want the solicitor to continue working for them because they have put the time and resources needed to train that person for the job.

However, if you are not awarded a position with the firm you did your training contract with, you will then need to prepare for your life as a solicitor by applying and interviewing with a new firm or organisation.

Once you have applied for a position in a firm, you will begin the interview process. While the experience will vary from one firm to another, the process is usually similar and will include multiple interviews.

It is important that you take a few steps before the interview process so that you are as prepared as possible and can impress those who are interviewing you.

Your interview is your chance to make the employer take notice of who you are and where you fit into their organisation. Be professional. Dress the part. Speak clearly and with an appropriate volume. Shake their hand firmly and smile. Don't talk to them like they are your friend, or they may not be your future employer. Show them that you are the right person to hire.

Things to remember for your interview

• **Extensively research the firm for which you are interviewing.** Use the internet to search not only their website, but to find other articles or write-ups about the firm. It is important that you know what field of law the company operate within, and any major cases that they may have worked on. It will give you an advantage over other candidate's if you show full knowledge and interest about the law firm for which you are applying to. You can also find out a little bit about the partners during this research, as well as their rankings in various practice areas.

• **Dress appropriately.** If you show up in jeans and a t-shirt, the partners may not feel you take the position seriously. Your clothing needs to demonstrate your professional and mature demeanour. For men, a suit shows that you are serious about the job and take pride in your appearance and how you convey yourself to others. For women, a skirted suit or conservative dress with a proper hemline will give the same effect. Be professional in your dress, and show up well groomed. These little details may seem simple, but they are important and extremely effective.

• **Familiarise yourself with some of the questions you may be asked during the interview process.** Some examples of questions you will be asked are: What makes you interested in our firm? Why are you interested in your stated area of practice? What are you hoping for in your career? What are your salary expectations?

Questions about salary expectations are generally the most difficult to answer. On one hand, you don't want to over-sell yourself, ask for too high a salary and get passed over because your demands can't be met. On the other hand, nobody wants to under-sell themselves and ask for too little. Finding a good balance is important.

Making yourself familiar with the common questions asked by an interviewer will help prepare you for your interview. Always remember to answer truthfully. Be prepared to answer tough questions confidently. Impress the interviewer with your knowledge of the firm for which you are applying, be personable, and take your time answering questions to ensure your answer is clear.

As you prepare for your interview, whether it be a phone interview or a face-to-face interview, you should ask yourself a few questions:

- What are the areas of law that you are really interested in and why?
- What can you offer the firm/organisation for which you are interviewing?
- Why do you want a career in law?
- Why did you decide to apply for this particular law firm/organisation?
- Would you prefer to work for a general firm, a high street firm or a commercial firm?

Asking yourself these questions will not only lead you towards firms who suit your own area of interest, but will help you to feel more comfortable with answering questions that are based specifically around your own experience. You might find a firm that you think you want to work for, but as you are researching and asking yourself the above questions, you may notice that it is not necessarily the best fit for you.

While researching the firms for which you are applying, it is also important to know when to stop. It will impress them that you researched them, but none of your interviewers will expect you to know everything about their firm. They just want to know that you have an interest in their firm and that you are ambitious and serious.

The STAR Method

The **STAR** method is one way you can prepare for an interview. It works most effectively when preparing responses to situational type interview questions.

The STAR method basically ensures that your responses to the interview questions follow a concise and logical sequence, and also ensures that you cover every possible area.

Situation – I will explain what the situation was and who else was involved. This will be a relatively detailed explanation, so that the interviewer fully understands the situation described.

Task – I will explain what the task was. This will be an explanation of what had to be done and by whom.

Action – I will then move on and explain what action I specifically took, and also what action other people took.

Result – I will finally explain what the outcome was following my actions. It is important to emphasise how your own actions, positively affected and resolved the end result of the issue.

This method can be utilised in any form of interview, whether that be a telephone interview, a face-to-face interview or a group interview. You need to demonstrate well-structured and logical responses. This method shows your ability to think carefully and intelligently, a highly attractive quality for employers.

Phone Interview

If you are using a recruiter to find your training contract or solicitor job, they will often conduct a phone interview. This serves as a tool for the recruiter to assess whether or not you are a serious applicant. During the phone interview they will know if they want to take you further through the application process. Unlike your second, and possibly third, interview, the phone interview will be used to focus on your general skills and competences. During the phone interview, it will be your goal to show your commitment and enthusiasm.

It is very important to be prepared. Make sure that you research and find out as much as possible about the recruiter. Also, read the job description for the position you are applying for and think about how you match the criteria. It is a good idea to write down any question you might have and also plan out your answers to the questions you think are likely to be asked. 'Tell me about yourself,' and 'What interests you about the job,' are very common and important questions that will be asked.

Practicing ahead of time will be a big help in preparing for your phone interview. Telesales and voluntary fundraising jobs will gain you crucial phone experience. If you feel you are lacking in experience using the phone in a professional context, ask a friend, relative or someone at your career centre to help you. Ask them for feedback on how you come across to them over the phone. Another great way to see how you sound to others would be to record yourself. While listening to yourself, you will be able to identify any potential issues and resolve them before the interview. Talking too quietly or quickly are potential issues that are easily corrected.

Make sure you are fully prepared for your phone interview. Do not take the phone interview in an environment that is loud, chaotic or overwhelming. Find a nice quiet place that allows you to gather your thoughts and act professional.

Taking control of your environment on the day of the interview is important. The telly should be off, as well as any music. If you have housemates, let them know what you are about to do and ask them to give you some privacy. You need to ensure that there will be no interruptions as this can and will be viewed as unprofessional. You will also want to have your notes/research nearby as well as a copy of your application or CV, a copy of the job description and any interview details. Sitting at a desk or table will help you to be organized and ready.

While it is natural to be nervous about your phone interview, it is important that you stay calm. Take a few deep breaths before you dial or answer your phone. When speaking, make sure you are clear and speaking at a reasonable pace. Don't rush to answer a question. If a question is tricky, it is perfectly acceptable to say, 'Let me just reflect on that for a moment,' and then take some time to think about your answer. If you are unclear about a question or if you didn't hear the entire question, it is fine to ask for some clarification.

Always be professional. Remember, this is just a preliminary step in the interview process. Feel free to ask your questions at the end of the interview. This is not the time for questions about salary, training and start dates. These issues will be addressed in further interviews.

Take notes during the interview, or write them down as soon as you hang up. Focus on writing down the questions that were asked and your answers. It will serve as a useful record for the next stage, if you are asked to come in for a personal interview.

Things to avoid during a telephone interview:

- **Background noise.** A quiet room is always better than a crowded café.

- **Chewing and gulping.** It is okay to have a glass of water near you to sip should your mouth go dry during the interview, but never eat or drink casually while taking part in an interview.

- **Multitasking.** You should never be replying to e-mail, making lunch, or checking Facebook. Focus only on the person who is speaking to you. They will know if you are distracted.

- **Taking other calls or responding to texts.** If you are using a landline phone, switch off your mobile phone and vice versa if you are using your mobile phone.

- **Being too laid back.** If you slouch on the couch, lie on your bed or lounge around, you will be less alert, less likely to focus and will sound uninterested. Sit up straight or take the call standing up; it will help you to stay alert and you will seem more confident to the caller.

On-Site Interview

If venturing out on your own to find a job, the first interview will be when the employer (either the partners, HR or both) will walk through your CV and possibly do a personality matching exercise.

If you are asked back for a second interview, this is where you will be asked more specific questions about your history, experience and skills. During this interview, you may be shown the offices and be introduced to the other solicitors and partners. If you are not introduced and shown around during this interview, you will most likely be called back for a third and less formal interview where you will be shown around.

While being introduced to others at the firm, it is important that you make a good impression on all employees of the firm. Good interactions with others will show HR and the partners that you are easy to get along with and would make a great addition to their team.

Other than relevant work experience, there are many other qualities that an employer will be looking for in a prospective solicitor. Make yourself aware of and comfortable with the following list of qualities, and ensure that a large number of them shine through during your interview:

- Dedication and commitment
- Excellent written and oral communication skills
- Accuracy and attention to detail, commercial awareness
- Numeracy skills
- Analytical skills
- Problem-solving skills
- Ability to prioritise and plan
- Negotiating skills
- IT skills
- Flexibility and openness to new ideas
- Excellent time management skills
- Professionalism
- Integrity
- Respect for confidentiality
- Stamina and resiliency

Because being a solicitor involves a lot of client contact, and because the client is placing their faith, confidence and trust in you, there are a number of things that an interviewer will be watching for during an interview to show them your level of professionalism. They want to ensure that you are the right person to manage their clients. Here is a list of areas that the interviewer will take note of during an interview:

- Your appearance
- Whether your interest in the law is real
- Whether you are articulate and able to think on your feet
- Whether you are a committed and serious candidate
- Your temperament and personality
- Your sense of humor
- Your level of initiative
- Your self-awareness

- How you will get along with the rest of their staff
- Whether or not your responses correspond or conflict with those on your CV or application
- How you are able to cope with pressure and deadlines
- Whether you display analytical, intellectual and reasoning ability
- Whether or not you would fit in with their organizational culture and structure
- Your attitude to working alone or with supervision
- Your organisational and time management skills

Interview Questions and Answers

Below are typical questions that you are likely to be asked during your interview. This chapter also contains sample answers of the responses which will improve your chances of successfully completing your interview.

1. Question: Why does this position interest you?

The interviewer wants to see a genuine enthusiasm in your answer. It is here that you should show what you can contribute to the firm.

'This job is a perfect match for my skills and career ambitions. I know I can be successful with your firm and at the same time, my successes will be rewarded.'

2. Question: You don't have any experience in litigation, is that correct?

You were shortlisted, so this obviously isn't a problem.

Instead of saying, 'No, I don't,' you could say, 'I don't yet have experience in litigation, but I would love to broaden my experience in this area. Because I am a fast learner and adapt well to new situations, I think litigation would be an exciting new experience for me that I could excel in.'

3. Question: What was your greatest challenge, and how did you overcome it?

You should have an example ready of a situation that brought you outside of your comfort zone and how you adapted. Make sure your example is relevant to the job.

'While undertaking my studies we did a mock-courtroom exercise and I briefly froze up when it came to speaking in front of a crowded room. By taking a few deep breaths and thinking about my next statement, I was able to overcome the fear and continue on to win my case.'

4. Question: What are your strengths?

If you had done research on the firm for which you are applying, then you will know what exactly they are looking for. Tailor your answer to fit and focus on what most interviewers seek; problem solving skills, teamwork, flexibility and motivation are all good examples to speak of. Focus on select matters rather than list a lot of strengths. By knowing what you have to offer them, you will be able to talk about it in a way that will keep the interviewer engaged.

'While I do work well on my own, I do have the ability to work in a group, both as a participant and as a leader. My motivation to help people who are unable to help themselves has helped me to become better at what I do, and I know that I am very flexible.'

5. Question: What is your biggest weakness?

The interviewer is asking this question to see if you are arrogant, whether you know yourself and how you are working to overcome a weakness.

'My colleagues have told me that I tend to be too focused on my work and that I need to remind myself to lighten up.'

Don't be tempted to use this question to be funny or to offer a real weakness. Besides the three reasons already listed for why this question is asked, the interviewer will ask this question because it helps them to see how you handle difficult situations.

6. Question: You have done a bit of job hopping, why?

'I moved companies so that I could progress in my career. I would much rather develop with a company whose values match my own,' would be an appropriate answer to this question.'

7. Question: Where do you see yourself in 10 years?

This is where you show the interviewer where this job fits into your goals and aspirations. Here you would explain how the job is an opportunity for you to grow and develop as a solicitor. Never bring up goals that are truly unrealistic.

'In 10 years I hope to see myself as a highly regarded partner, and hopefully, growing and developing with this firm will allow me to do that here.'

8. Question: Do you prefer working on your own or on a team?

Unless you know it is a team job or an individual job, it is better to just say that you enjoy both.

'I enjoy working both on my own and as a team. I understand that working for a large firm like yours allows me to be both on my own and contributing to the firm in a team environment, and that is one of the reasons why I desire a position with this firm.'

9. Question: Why are you interested in leaving your current job?

Never say anything negative about your current company.

'I am at a stage in my career where I want a job that is more challenging and rewarding,' 'The company values are a closer match for me here,' 'The firm I work for is much too far from where I live and I am looking for a shorter commute.'

These are all appropriate answers for this particular question.

10. Question: Why should I hire you over the other people I have interviewed?

This is, again, where the interviewer wants to see your confidence. Be proud of your accomplishments without bragging.

'You mentioned you are looking for someone with proven experience and who is motivated. I am ideal for this position because with my previous experience I can step in and make an immediate contribution.'

11. Question: What do you know about us?

This is another chance for you to impress the interviewer. Show them that you took the initiative to research the company. Referring to their annual report or how they are expanding will show the interviewer that you have researched the firm and like what you have learned.

'During my research, I found that your rate of expansion was extremely high. What this tells me is that your firm is successful and not going anywhere any time soon. With such growth, this is definitely someplace I could see myself.'

12. Question: If you could choose any job, what would it be?

This is not where you start describing your fantasy job. Here you would describe the job you are being interviewed for. (In this sample case, the position is for a trainee finance solicitor.)

'At this point in my career, I see myself growing in the world of finance law. Being a part of the team here, I feel that I would not only be an asset to your firm, but would gain the knowledge and experience in finance law that I am seeking.'

13. Question: Would you be willing to relocate?

This is an important question. Think about this in advance so that you can answer honestly.

'At this point in my life, I am definitely open to the possibility of relocating,' or, 'Due to obligations outside of work, I wouldn't feel comfortable with the possibility of relocating.'

14. Question: Would you accept this job if it was offered to you?

Without hesitation, answer yes. There is always time for negotiations later.

'Absolutely. I applied for this position because I am impressed with the work that this firm does, and would love the opportunity to be a part of your team.'

15. Question: What would be the area you feel least confident about if we offered you a job?

You are being tested on your self-confidence with this question.

'With my willingness and ability to learn new things quickly, along with my determination and dedication, I feel I would do great in this position.'

This would be an acceptable answer. Expand on your strengths and what you can bring to the table. Let them know you are looking forward to this new role should they offer.

16. Question: What are you like at time management?

Time management is a skill that not everyone possesses, but is crucial when it comes to applying for jobs. Being able to manage your time effectively is imperative, and you must be able to demonstrate your time management qualities and professionalism.

'I am very effective at time management. I am the type of person who is extremely organised and knows what they want to achieve during each day. I like to keep lists, which act as a reminder of what I want to achieve and in what timeframe. For example, if I have a busy schedule planned for the forthcoming week, I will always write down what I want to during that week. This allows me to plan ahead and makes sure that I have everything in place so that I can achieve each objective'.

17. Question: Why should we give you the job?

You need to give the interview an answer that benefits them and not just yourself. Yes of course you are the best person for the job, but don't say it unless you can back it up with examples of why. Here are a few examples of why you might be the best person for the job:

- You have the ability to work in a fast-changing environment that requires commitment, drive and enthusiasm.

- You are capable of achieving great things for their firm and thrive under pressurised situations. For example, in your previous role you were given a deadline of three days to achieve a highly complex task that required high levels of motivational skills. You brought the team together, briefed them on what was expected and monitored each stage of progress carefully.

- You can make a positive impact on the overall environment in which you work, and are dependable in every situation to deliver what is required.

- You are a team player who has the experiences and skills to match the job description.

- You are loyal, hardworking and will act as a positive role model for their firm.

18. Question: What are the missions and aims of our firm?

Law firms like to see that you have extensively researched their firm, and taken it upon yourself to gather up as much information as possible. Many firms set themselves aims and objectives. There are sometimes in the form of a vision or charter. They usually relate to the high level of customer service that they promise to deliver. When you apply for any role you should not only prepare for each stage of the selection process, but you should also learn as much as you regarding each firm. Leading this kind of information is important and will demonstrate your seriousness about joining their particular firm.

19. Question: What makes a good leader?

In order to become a good leader, you must have a number of different skills that you can draw upon, and these include:

- **Being a visionary** – an ability to see the end result or the desired goal.

- **Provide inspiration** – great leaders need to be capable of inspiring their team towards a goal or objective.

- **Strategic thinker** – being able to think outside the box and plan for the future.

- **Being liked by the team** – whilst not essential, it certainly helps to be liked by your team. If they like you, they will follow you.

- **Being an effective decision maker** – having the ability to make decisions, ever sometimes unpopular ones.

- **Accepting of feedback and criticism** – good leaders should be able to take criticism from others. This will help them to continually improve.

20. Question: Do you need other people around to stimulate you, or are you self-motivated?

Most employers want their staff to be self-motivated. If an employee is self-motivated, then he or she are going to perform to a high standard. Job satisfaction is vital if a person is going to perform well at work.

Your response to this question should focus on providing examples of whether you have been self-motivated in a current or previous work role. It is easy for an interviewee to say that they are self-motivated, but proving it will examples is a different matter.

'Whilst I enjoy working in a team environment, I am a highly self-motivated person. I don't like it when I'm sat around doing nothing,

so I'm always on the lookout for new things to do. That applied to when I'm either at home or at work. For example, in my last job, I wanted to look for ways to improve the company turnover. Without being asked, I set about researching different areas that that the company could potentially draw more income streams from. I contacted a number of potential customers and arranged to send them some company literature. My manger was very pleased with the fact that I'd been self-motivated enough to try to make a positive difference.'

The following few pages gives you some room to draft some answers for the main questions that you can expect to answer during your interview.

Why do you want to work for our firm?

Tell me, what do you already know about the firm?

Tell me about yourself?

What can you bring to our firm that makes you stand out from other lawyers?

What is your biggest strength? What would you say your biggest weakness is?

Where do you see yourself in 5 years' time?

Questions YOU can ask

Many people don't take into consideration the idea of asking the interviewer questions during the interview. It is more than acceptable to find out as much as you can about the position you are interviewing for. It will show the interviewer that you are very interested and that you like to take initiative. Nobody likes to waste their time, and HR/Partners are no exception to that rule. If you ask questions now and find out that the position isn't for you, it saves them the time to train you, only for you to find out later that you want out. Asking questions to find out more about the job makes you look good and is a win-win for all involved.

- Could you please share with me some of the details about the department or the law firm's culture?

- How would you describe the individuals who are successful in this position? What characteristics or qualities do they have?

- How will my performance be evaluated? How often? By whom will I be evaluated?

- What is your firm's management style?

- Where will my opportunities lie within your firm over the next five years knowing my commitment to working hard and demonstrating my legal skills and abilities?

- What does your firm do to contribute to its employees' professional development?

- What are the biggest challenges I would face in this position?

- How has your firm addressed the issue of the most recent change in court rules and how will it affect your firm directly? (This would work with a recent change in regulation or appellate decision as well. It will show that you are up on current events and show them that you have done your homework.)

- What is the next step in the process?

Questioning Techniques

How you present yourself during that all important interview is crucial. You want to convey yourself in a professional and mature manner in order for law firms to take you seriously. Remember, you've worked hard to get to this point. You don't want to mess up your interview stage because you lacked the correct technique in your interview.

REMEMBER: It's what you **don't say** that counts.

← Trimmed haircut
← Clean shaved
← Formal dress
← Warm smile
← Correct upright body posture
← Firm handshake
← Feel of confidence

Tips for Your Law Interview

- **Dress to impress.** As mentioned multiple times already, your first impression is extremely important. Unless you are informed that the interview is casual, you should be prepared to wear a suit.

- **Read your CV, cover letter and application the night before.** The interviewer will be asking questions regarding the content. If there have been any changes or additions since you turned these items in, bring the new information with you. Any new experience could be the difference between getting the job and leaving without it.

- **Be aware of your body language.** No matter how nervous you may be, or how stumped a question may have left you, let them see you as a confident and composed individual.

- **Greet each person you meet with a firm handshake and excellent eye contact.** While the strength of your handshake will not determine how well you could do the job, it will add to a list of things that the employer will be keeping in mind as the build their perception of you. Don't overdo it, though. Broken fingers on the hand of your interviewer will not bode well for you either.

- **From the moment you walk into the interview to the moment you leave, assume you are being tested.** This means that you should be friendly and polite to everyone you come in contact with. Always think before you speak. Interviewers want to see that you are well spoken.

- **Plan your journey.** It is important to know the route to the job interview. This will help you to get there ahead of schedule. Showing up late will not help your chances of landing a job.

- **The delivery of your answers is very important.** Excessive one word answers, as well as rambling on and on about your life will not be seen as appropriate. You want to be seen as a person who can formulate smart, concise responses. After all, you will be speaking on behalf of your clients once you land your job.

- **Know what questions you want to ask your interviewer.** It is perfectly acceptable to bring in a note of your questions. It will let the interviewer know that you have thought about the job ahead of time and that you are interested in knowing more. Make sure to listen to everything the interviewer says during the interview so that when you ask your questions you are not asking about something that has already been said.

- **Look engaged.** Sitting forward and taking control of your facial expressions and nervous gestures will be important. You don't want to be fiddling or compulsively moving your feet and hands. Steady breathing can be used to calm your nerves.

- **Smile**. Not only will smiling make you feel more relaxed, but it will help you to build a nice rapport with your interviewer.

- **Don't attempt to fill awkward silences**, especially when the interviewer is looking at your CV.

- **Make sure that you listen** to the interviewers question in its entirety before attempting to answer.

- **If there is more than one interviewer, make sure that you make eye contact with each person as you answer questions**, but always give the lion's share of the eye contact to the person who asked the question.

- **At the end of the interview, always thank the interviewer(s)** for their time, smile and shake their hand. Offer a polite goodbye on your way out.

How to Cope With Rejection

Almost everybody who interviews will face rejection at one point or another in life. Sure, there are some that always seem to succeed, no matter what challenge is put in front of them, but those are just a few who are the exception to the rule. Whether you are used to rejection or not, it doesn't make it any easier. Obviously rejection is something we would all love to avoid. Be strong, and use the rejection as a learning experience.

Because the interview process isn't perfect, it is easy for anyone to feel that they aced the interview. Just like you, the interviewers have their own flaws, likes and dislikes. While you have all of the skills and abilities to do well in the position, they may have already had a set type of person in their mind, and you may not have fit in that picture. Because you can't possibly know what vision they have for the prospective hire, it is up to you to understand and move on.

Keep in mind, however, that there is still hope. If you feel that the interview went really well and yet you still got the call to tell you that you didn't get the job, there is something you can do. Feel free to call the employer and let them know how impressed you were with them at the interview. You can also let them know that you would be very interested should the candidate they chose not work out. Also tell them that if another similar position opened up that you would, again, be very interested. By doing this, they may know somebody else that you would be a good fit with.

Ask For Feedback:

If you were not offered a position after what you felt was a successful interview, it is totally acceptable for you to contact the recruiting department of the firm and ask for feedback. It is advisable to speak to somebody who did not take part in the interview, but sometimes that cannot be avoided depending on the size of the firm.

When asking for feedback, it is important for you to keep calm, be polite and be as brief as possible. Also remember to not argue with them if you disagree with what they are telling you. Listen carefully and take notes. You are getting this feedback so that you know what to improve on for your next interview.

The most common reason you will encounter for why you did not get an offer is that you lacked the necessary skills or knowledge. Often this happens when you are applying for a job that is higher than what you are actually qualified for. Adjusting your expectations and applying for a job a little lower on the career ladder may help you get a job you are actually qualified for.

Another reason you may not have gotten the position could be that your interview skills need attention. Showing your nerves can sometimes be mistaken as you being unfriendly. If you were nervous so much causing your communication skills to suffer, you may want to try practising before the next interview. Not only will this help calm your nerves, but any feedback you get in the practice interview will definitely be helpful.

If you are given a generic excuse for why you did not get an offer, such as, 'You didn't have enough experience,' or, 'We went with a more qualified candidate,' feel free to ask which skills or qualifications you were lacking. Listen carefully to what skills they would have liked to have seen you display. This is your chance to learn more of what employers are expecting. If they choose to not give you any detailed reasons, it is best to accept what they have told you and thank them again.

There will also be times when a recruiter will not give you any feedback. If this is the case, you will have no choice but to just move forward and try again with another firm. Other times, you may be pleasantly surprised when asking for feedback. You may find out that the person who beat you out for the position did so very narrowly. If this is the case, the employer may let you know that they will be keeping your information on file so that they can contact you as soon as another position opens.

No matter the reason for not being offered a position, don't let it discourage you. Use it as a learning experience, improve upon yourself and keep trying.

Being Put on Hold

Under normal circumstances, if you are the right person for the job, you will be offered a position almost immediately. With the current state of the economy, you may find yourself being put on hold. While this means that you have not yet been offered a position, it doesn't mean that you won't be offered a position. This is actually a good thing, because had you not been a good candidate, you would have been rejected instantly.

There are some things you can do when you have been put on hold:

• **Keep applying for other jobs and going to interviews.** You should not assume that you have gotten the job; you may not get it and will have wasted precious time that could have been used to possibly land an even better position.

• **While waiting to hear back about the position that is on hold, keep in touch with the recruiter.** Make sure they know that you are still very interested in the position.

CHAPTER 14

Law Assessment Centres

What are Law Assessment Centres?

Law Assessment Centres are another method that large law firms will use in their quest to find the perfect candidate or candidate. Generally, they are two days long and involve a series of tests, exercises and interviews. These activities are designed to measure your competency for a trainee position.

Assessment Centres are very expensive, so individuals are usually sent to them at the very end of a training contract or vacation scheme, to ensure that they are competent enough to carry on in the firm. If you have been invited to attend an Assessment Centre, it means you have already done well and the firm is willing to take on the extra cost to make absolutely sure that you are the right person for the job.

Why are Law Assessment Centres used?

Assessment Centres are believed to be the most accurate way to recruit trainees. Because you are actually taking part in an activity, you are able to show your skills rather than just talk about them.

Moreover, Law Assessment Centres are used in order to evaluate a candidate's competencies regarding the knowledge and skills required for a lawyer. They are primarily used so candidates are able to show what they are capable of. It is a way of putting everything they have learned prior to the assessment, into action.

An Assessment Centre is used to decipher strong candidate's. The important thing to remember regarding the Assessment Centre is that if you think you did not perform well at one task, you can impress in other areas.

How to prepare for a Law Assessment Centre?

The preparation process for attending a Law Assessment course, is similar to that of a job interview. You should conduct large amounts of research prior to both. You need to know what the selection criteria are, come up with questions that you may want to ask about the law firm, and ask those questions when you meet with current employees at any professional event.

There are multiple exercises that you will be required to participate in. Each activity and exercise will test you on different abilities, strengths and skills. On the following pages you will find a group of the most common exercises performed at law Assessment Centres as well as a description of what each exercise helps a recruiter look for.

Role play exercise: This may involve a mock telephone call with a client, a mock hearing or an interaction with another solicitor.

It usually tests your ability to retain information, negotiate and communicate with anyone you may come in contact with as a solicitor.

Face-to-face Interview: You will take part in actual interviews with a professional and a member of the HR team.

A timed legal-based written exercise: To test your legal knowledge and understanding

Report writing task: To test your written communication skills.

Competency-based Interview: One-to-one interview lasting up to an hour. You will be asked questions to assess your competence in communication skills, organisational skills, goal- setting, problem solving, teamwork and commercial awareness.

Group exercises: During your time at the law Assessment Centre, you will most likely encounter one form of group exercise or another. This might involve a debate, a mock-meeting, a role-play situation or a problem solving exercise. These activities are geared towards showing not only your ability to lead, but your ability to work as a team. Working well with others is a must if you want to be considered for a position as a solicitor.

Presentations: You may be asked to give a presentation to a small group of people. The subject may have been given to you ahead of time or that day.

Psychometric tests: These tests will include non-verbal reasoning, verbal reasoning and critical thinking exercises. Only some firms do this during Assessment Centre activities, others do it prior to the Assessment Centre.

In-tray or e-tray exercise: This task will test whether you can make important decisions under pressure and on a deadline.

What is included in an Assessment Centre?

The types of exercises you will take at your assessment are typical of that of a trainee solicitor. All of these exercises are used to reflect the type of work you are likely to face in a regular work day.

A Law Assessment Centre uses an array of exercises and assessments in the hopes of gaining an overall picture of your performance. The following areas are typical areas that are likely to be used within your assessment:

➤ Psychometric Tests

While all areas that will be covered at a Law Assessment Centre are important, the psychometric tests will tell the law firm the most about you. These tests are used to identify a candidate's ability, aptitudes and/or personality. While you will find that most psychometric tests are done online, there are still some that are done as hard-copy questionnaires.

Generally, there are two types of psychometric tests, personality tests and aptitude or ability tests. Personality tests are used to identify a personal type. There are no wrong answers. Usually, they will involve paired items and you will be asked to choose which one you prefer. These tests need to be answered honestly and without trying to guess the "right" answer since there is no right answer.

Aptitude or ability tests are designed to assess your cognitive ability and reasoning. Generally speaking, these tests are timed and include numerical tests, subject/job-specific tests, verbal and reasoning tests.

It is important that you read all of the instructions carefully, don't try to guess the right answers, work through briskly and accurately, answer honestly and pay attention to what you are being asked. Do not dwell on the answer for long, and answer the next question if you are stuck. You can find practice tests online at multiple sites. It is possible that some organisations will charge for the practice tests. It is also possible that the website for the firm you are applying to will provide practice testing and coaching on how to improve your scores.

To get FREE access to psychometric tests which will help you prepare for your solicitor assessment centre, go to:
www.MyPsychometricTests.com

▶ Face-to-Face Interview

This is like any other interview that you have had to sit before. You will normally be interviewed by a qualified member of the law profession and a member of the HR department.

You need to make sure that you are well prepared and are fully competent with answering questions based on your application. Before your interview, make sure you have made thorough notes and revise your answers before attending your assessment. You want to make a good impression, and you do not want to be let down by your lack of preparation.

Details of how to prepare for a successful interview, can be found in the 'Interview' chapter. This chapter will provide you with detailed answers that you can use to answer some of the most common questions used in the interview process.

▶ Report Writing

Foremost, this test is used to assess your written communication skills. As a lawyer, it is imperative that you are able to show high levels of communication, both verbally and written.

➤ In-Tray or E-Tray Exercise

In-Tray or E-Tray tests have become a popular way of assessing a candidate's performance. This test is designed to test a person's ability to show great levels of prioritising and organising. As a lawyer, you will be expected to prioritise your day depending on the cases and issues that need dealing with first. You will need to show proficiency and demonstrate your ability to make decisions in pressurised situations.

➤ Role Play Exercises

A Role Play assessment is exactly what it says: playing a role within a given situation. This could include a mock hearing or a telephone call with a client or solicitor. These tests are formally used to put you in the shoes of a real life scenario: a scenario which you are likely to face as a trainee solicitor.

A role play exercise is used to assess your communication skills and determine how well you can perform within a role. Other key skills that are assessed in this exercise are:

• Your ability to retain information
• Your negotiating skills
• Your professionalism
• Your skills, knowledge and persona

➤ Group Exercises

You are more than likely to experience a group assessment. This could take some form of role play (as mentioned above), debates, mock-meetings or a problem-solving exercise.

Recruiters will not only be looking at your ability to work in a group and 'hold your own ground', but also to demonstrate levels of leadership, interaction, professionalism, individual determination and sheer passion for committing to the job.

▶ Presentations

Some Law Assessment centres may require you to complete a presentation in front of a small group of people. You may be notified of a topic before your assessment, or asked to put a presentation together on the day of your assessment. Either way, you need to demonstrate your knowledge, skills and determination to successfully complete a presentation, whether rehearsed or not.

Helpful Assessment Centre Tips

- **Prepare:** It is really important that you know about the firm you are hoping to work for on a permanent basis. You should know the areas of law that the firm specialises in, any large cases that the firm has worked on recently and the location of their offices. If the law firm tells you the names of the partners that will be doing the assessing, you should take the time to research those partners and at least know the area of law that they practice.

- **Be punctual:** As a general rule, you should try to be about five minutes early when going to a law Assessment Centre. If you arrive late, you will be flustered and it will not bode well with the law firm. If you arrive extra early, do not go into the Assessment Centre. The assessors will not be prepared for you and it will only cause you to become more anxious.

- **Practice:** While you have no way of knowing exactly what exercises you will be doing on assessment days, you can practice. Many careers services can help you by providing you with psychometric tests and practice written exercises. Since these practice exercises may not be exactly the ones you will be doing on assessment day, what they will really be preparing you for is the format and speed at which you will have to perform. You can also look at the job application and the 'what we are looking for' section of their website to know what skills they are looking for. Most likely, they will be assessing you on those skills.

- **Stay current:** Knowing what is going on in the world of news and legal press will help you prepare. Presentation topics, case study materials and interview questions have a good chance of coming from something that has been in the news recently. This will also help you prove your commercial awareness.

- **Read everything they give you:** When a law firm sends you to an Assessment Centre, they will likely provide you with a pack of information about the day/days. Read it thoroughly because it may include the exercises you will be doing, people you will be meeting and logistics such as where the Assessment Centre will be and what times are involved. Also, it is possible that in the information there will be tasks that you will need to do beforehand, such as prepare a presentation. Should you not be prepared and are unable to participate in one of the exercises, you could lose a valuable training contract or vacation scheme.

- **Find out more:** Since there will most likely be current employees at the Assessment Centre, you have a great opportunity to learn more about the law firm. Any chance you get, ask questions. Find out why they like working there. That will help you to find out if you are looking at the right firm to work for.

- **Be well-rested:** Assessment Centres tend to be quite exhausting, so get plenty of rest the night before.

- **Don't take control:** While recruiters love to see that you have strong leadership qualities, there is a time and place for that. In the group activities, it is important to work as a group and give all group members a fair chance. After all, you are all there in the activity to succeed at the task they give you.

- **Don't get discouraged:** If you feel as though you didn't do well in one exercise, don't give up. These Assessment Centres are designed to show your strengths. It is extremely rare that recruiters find applicants that excel in every exercise. Just keep your head up and try your best in the next exercise.

- **Be yourself:** Do not try to be something you are not. During these assessments, it is almost impossible to act your way through them, and trying to do so will just make things more complicated. Let your personality be what makes you stand out from the crowd. Individuality will show the recruiters that you aren't just a cookie-cutter body but a person with the ability to shine.

CHAPTER 15

THE JOB OFFER

Aside from completing your legal studies, being offered a job is one of the best moments of your solicitor career. You have worked very hard to get to this point. But the hard work doesn't end here. Now comes the time to seal your job offer. Now the new stress comes in regarding how to deal with the job offer. *Do you want to accept it or decline it? It is the right job for you? Is the job offer somewhere where you can see yourself working?* It may seem like a simple choice, but there is a specific way that things must be done. You must know how an offer is made, and what that entails.

No matter if a job offer is conditional or unconditional, it should always be made in writing. If you have been verbally told that you are being offered the position, you should still expect to get the offer in writing. You will receive an official offer letter. Sometimes this letter will come alone, and other times it will also include a copy of the terms and conditions of employment. This is known as a 'formal employment contract'.

Before signing the contract, it is important to do proper checks to make sure that everything is how you expect it to be and that you are happy with the offer and its conditions.

You will want to check:

- Job title
- Salary and benefits
- Hours of work and Start date
- The notice period (what they have to give you and what you have to give them)
- Holiday and sick pay entitlements

Before signing, you should be aware of the fact that the offer is binding. Jumping into a contract without fully understanding it, ties you to a job you may not being happy with. If you don't understand something on the letter or contract, you should contact the employer and get clarification as soon as possible. This should also be done if the contract isn't as was discussed verbally, such as pay or location of the job. If any changes are made to the contract, you should be sent a revised copy.

If you are offered a job right out of the gates, but still have some interviews to attend, never fear. Most large graduate recruiters will understand and will not necessarily expect an instant acceptance. This being said, you still need to contact them promptly. You can write to them so as to acknowledge the offer, but indicate when you will get back to them with your decision. Be professional in your response and never say that you are waiting to see if you get a better offer. It is best to keep in touch with the recruiter so that they know you are still interested.

All of your hard work has finally paid off. Take the time to congratulate yourself and be proud of your accomplishments.

If all is well with the offer and you are absolutely sure that the offer and the job is what you want, you will need to accept in writing. If you have received more than one job offer, it is best to take your time in deciding which position fits you best. Automatically jumping for the highest paying of the offers may come back to bite you later. Make sure that everything that the firm is offering makes you comfortable. Keep job development, size of the firm, work schedule, workload, potential to advance and location in mind when deciding which offer suits you best.

On the following page you will find a sample acceptance of job offer letter. Keep in mind that there are various ways that the letter could be worded, but that the sample is a basic format to show you how simple the letter should be:

XXX Law Firm
012 Unnamed Road
Leicester
LE1 1XX
01 May 2014

Dear Ms. Mayfield,

I would like to thank you very much for offering me the Trainee Solicitor position with your firm. I would also like to let you know that I feel it will be a great privilege to work for such a prestigious law firm.

I am delighted to accept your offer. I have read over the contract and acknowledge that my starting annual salary will be £43,000 with a review in six months, at which time my salary will be heightened to £51,500 if I meet all standards. I also understand that the additional benefits offered will begin 28 days after my employment commences.

I would like to express my gratitude, once again, for your offer and I look forward to 15 May 2014 as my first day of employment.

Sincerely,

Charlotte Bloomfield
456 My Street
Birmingham
B17 6NF

Negotiating Your Employment Package

While some contracts are non-negotiable, others leave room for you to negotiate. Keep in mind that when negotiating salary, it is best to do your research ahead of time. You don't want to undersell yourself, and you most definitely do not want to oversell yourself.

By researching the employer and the market, you will be able to familiarise yourself with not only the company making the offer, but with what other competitors also offer. Here are five things to do when researching your salary:

- Talk to people in your professional and personal network.
- Ask for advice from a contact in the industry.
- Look at packages offered for similar positions online or in the jobs pages.
- If you are a member of a union, they can advise you on some acceptable salaries.
- Talk to your local Training and Enterprise Council.

You can easily lose an offer if you ask for more than the position deserves. At the same time, asking too little can also put off a prospective employer. By using the above stated resources, you can educate yourself about the current market and make an informed pitch.

Another thing to consider when negotiating your contract is the benefits package. You may find that accepting a slightly lower amount may not be a bad thing, if the benefits that are offered are exceptional.

You may also be able to negotiate a pay raise after a specific amount of time with the firm. If their base rate is lower than you had expected, but you can get them to agree to a set pay raise after an allotted amount of time, this is also a positive thing to consider.

There are three common mistakes that people make in salary negotiations:

- **Lack of research.** If you ask for more than what the firm is offering, they are likely to ask why you think you deserve the amount.
  If you don't have enough facts to back up the amount you're
  asking for, you will likely be passed over.

- **Bluffing.** If you try to convince the firm that you got a better offer
  from another firm and it is not true, you will likely be found out.
  Many recruiters communicate with one another and they will be
  able to confirm whether or not you are bluffing quite easily.

- **Too much interest in the package offered.** If you are showing
  more interest in the money you will make than in the position you
  are being offered, the recruiter will feel that you aren't serious about
  being a solicitor for the right reasons. You must find a balance.

Starting Your New Job

While this time in your life may be exciting, it can also be difficult to
get used to. You spent a lot of time in university, then spent the time
applying and interviewing for jobs, and now you are ready to get to
work. The following are some guidelines that may help you in your
transition:

- **What to wear?** If you were looking for an excuse to go shop-
  ping, this would be one. It is important that you have the proper
  wardrobe for your new job. Look back on how the interviewer/
  interviewers were dressed. This is a good place to start in planning your wardrobe. Your first day on the job will be better served
  if you are dressed conservatively. If you get to work and you find
  that you are overdressed, then the next day you can adjust for
  that. You don't want to show up to your first day in shorts to find
  everyone else in suits and ties.

- **Go back over your research.** If you followed previous directions,
  you will have a wealth of knowledge in the notes you have taken

and the research you have done about the firm you are now a part of. Go back over that research. Familiarise yourself with the firm all over again. You can even phone your new boss and ask them if there is any addition material that would be helpful to you.

- **Be friendly and put your best face forward.** As stated previously, first impressions are everything. Stay professional, but get to know your colleagues; this will build a good working environment. Show that you are approachable, helpful and that you are happy to be there.

- **Organsie effectively.** Make sure you know exactly what is expected of you. Knowing how the firm prefers to communicate (phone, face-to-face, email, memos, etc.) is something you should find out from the beginning. Talk to your boss to find out the organisational structure of the firm as well as how your job relates to others. Knowing your place will take you far. It is time to do your job and do it well.

CHAPTER 16

CONCLUSION

By reaching the end of the guide, no doubt you will be ready to begin the preparation for becoming a solicitor.

Now is a great time to put all this information and advice into action and begin your long and eventful journey into the legal sector. The world of law and legal aid has changed considerably over the last few years, and I have no doubt that it will continue to change in the future.

I would like to thank you for purchasing this guide, and taking the time to read it. I have had great pleasure writing how to become a solicitor, and I hope that you are able to achieve your goal in pursing your career as a solicitor.

Good luck and best wishes.

HELPFUL RESOURCES

I have also created a blog in regards to becoming a solicitor in hope to provide more details in relation to salaries, law firms, universities and other useful information. For more information on these areas, please visit the following web link for further details: **www.solicitor-resources.co.uk.**

Thank you for reading how to become a solicitor. I hope that you have found this an invaluable guide and would like to wish you all the best with your future endeavours.